Country Wheelwright

Country
Wheelwright

JOCELYN BAILEY

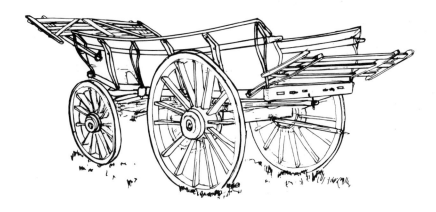

B.T. BATSFORD LTD LONDON

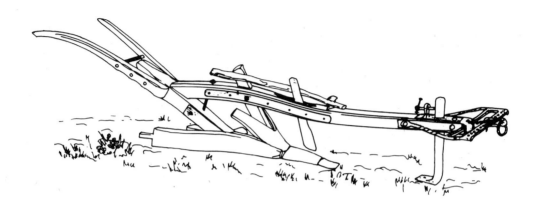

First published 1978
Copyright Jocelyn Bailey 1978

Filmset in 11/13 pt. Garamond by
Servis Filmsetting Ltd, Manchester

Printed in Great Britain by
The Anchor Press Ltd, Tiptree, Essex
for the Publishers B.T. Batsford Ltd,
4 Fitzhardinge Street, London W1H 0AH

ISBN 0 7134 1563 0

Contents

Acknowledgments

The author is pleased to record thanks to the following for their invaluable help: The Worshipful Company of Wheelwrights; the Curators and Staff of the Museum of English Rural Life, University of Reading; Folkestone Museum; Weald and Downland Open Air Museum; Wye College Agricultural Museum; Folkestone Public Library; *Kentish Express*; *Farnham Herald*; Croford Coach-builders; Kingsnorth Trailer Company; the family of the late Norman Heathfield; the family of the late Sydney Wheeler; Mary Dash; George Dutton; John Ferridge; Richard Filmer; Ted Hayward; Ernest Leithes; Arthur and Margaret Plewis; Len Primmer; Jim Rootes; George Stagg; John Thompson; Richard Walker; Ivor Warne; to all family members and those who have been involved in the day-to-day matters connected with the writing of this book, and to Bert who has described the craft details so patiently for recording.

The author and publishers would like to thank the following for the photographs and drawings used in this book: University of Reading, Museum of English Rural Life for figs 1, 6, 7, 8, 9, 10, 12, 13, 14, 18, 35, 36, 39, 48, 81, 82, 83; Richard Filmer for figs 61, 62, 63; Ted Hayward for fig. 4; Arthur Plewis for figs 68, 69, 70, 71, 72, 73; John Thompson for figs 15, 20; Richard Walker for fig. 16.

The author also wishes to thank those who kindly gave permission to photograph privately owned and museum items as noted in the captions. These photographs and the remaining illustrations are from the author's collection.

List of Illustrations

1   One of the set of press photographs taken at the Kingsnorth shop in 1925.
Shows Dad on the right, and the late Arthur Gaunt on the left. Arthur was
apprenticed to Dad, and worked for twenty-five years at the shop

CHAPTER 1

'A Dying Craft'

JUST OVER fifty years ago a press photographer called in to a country wheel-wright's shop in East Kent to take pictures and get a story. A photograph duly appeared in a national daily newspaper, with this caption:

A DYING INDUSTRY – One of the few remaining wheelwrights in the Home Counties pursuing his skilled craft at Kingsnorth, Kent. The trade has been handed down for generations, but the dwindling of British agriculture has reduced the demand for wagon wheels to a negligible quantity.

That wheelwright was the author's father-in-law, Albert E. Bailey ('Dad') and he took the wording of the caption as some sort of joke, for afterwards he often referred to himself as 'The Dying Craftsman'.

At the time Bert, his son, would have been about four years old, but later on Dad ignored the 'dying craft' idea by passing on to Bert the crafts of wheel-wrighting and carpentry.

Largely because of Dad's refusal to yield to the demands of the changing times, the old workshop and the family's outlook still retain more of the heritage of an older way of life than might normally be possible. Not that cords and gaiters are worn, but the many very close links with the past seem to be almost unbelievable. To collect a day's supply of kindling wood which has been chopped on the large elm block – so typical of a wheelwright's shop – and which was given to Bert by the late Mr Heathfield when the Heathfield wheelwrighting shop in nearby Ashford closed in 1954, always brings to mind some little thing about the craft – perhaps half-remembered from George Sturt's book *The Wheelwright's Shop*, or something which Bert has discussed. (Another pleasant recollection is that James Arnold has portrayed one of Mr Heathfield's Kent waggons in his book *The Farm Waggons of England and Wales*.) Other relics in the shop have mainly family associations. The wheel stool must be a couple of centuries old; its origins are lost, and it looked ancient even when Dad was a boy. Such tools as the samson, spoke dog, augers and adzes also hold their secrets of antiquity: secrets of this woodland craft and the quiet simplicity of country life; of the hardships endured by un-complaining country folk who lived through one agricultural depression after another.

Within the writer's household it is the little things about the past which remain so vivid. For example, the point of how Dad liked to have a really deep layer of wood shavings all over the shop floor and abhorred it if anyone should sweep them up, seems of closer interest, somehow, than the realization that the family has witnessed the ebb-tide of a craft which was once so busy a part of village life.

However, to start at what was probably the beginning of the family's own history within this craft. During a visit to the Folkestone Public Library, the author enquired about reference books relating to the wheelwright's craft. It was immediately obvious that the librarian himself was most interested in the subject. When he learnt that the family's name in the craft was Maplesden, he soon unearthed a Bagshaw's directory of 1847 which had the name entered under the same village, practising the same craft. So far, no earlier reference has been found, but that library visit brought increased family interest in picturing the past of the craft.

The next piece of 'evidence' is an account book which has survived the years. It is dated in the 1860's and '70's. Chronologically, the next piece of material is an

Haberdashers, Rev. W. Toke, Edward Godfrey, Esq., Mr. Daniel Swaffer, Mr. Stephen Hart, Mr. James G. Meers, Miss Fanny Barton, and others

The Church (St. Michael) is a venerable fabric, with nave, chancel, and square tower: in the chancel is a handsome tomb inlaid with beautiful brasses, to the memory of Humphrey Clarke. The living is a rectory, valued in the King's books at £11 9s. 9½d., in the gift of J. Alliston, Esq., and incumbency of the Rev. Richard Baldock. The tithes were commuted, in 1839, for £635, extraordinary charge on hop grounds 15s. per acre. There are 21 acres of glebe in the parish. Three acres of land left by Humphrey Clarke, is now let for £4 per annum, and the amount carried to the churchwarden's account.

Baldock Rev. Richard, Rectory	Moore Daniel, shopkeeper
Bingham John, blacksmith	Theobald Wm. wheelwright & vict.
Harnden George, bricklayer	Queen's Head
Hughes Robert, grocer	Venner Wm. shoemaker
Maplesden George, wheelwright	Washford Jerry, farrier
Meers Jas Gray, corn factor & miller,	West Daniel, parish clerk
Chipley Hatch	

Farmers.		
Apps John	Dray William	Hope Wm. Mill bank
Banks Dd. Halfway hs	Hart Stephen, Park	Lawrence Thomas
Barton John	Hilder Edw, Ct lodge	Meers Jas Gray, Chipley
Barton Rd. (grazier)	Hilder Thos. Pound	Hatch
Bingham James	Hilder Thos Paine, But-	Pentecost Richard
Bishop Stephen, Brisley	tersland	Swaffer Daniel & Son,
Butcher John, Pilham	Hills Thos. Courtley	Munford

2   Bagshaw's Directory, 1847. List in the section on Kingsnorth includes George Maplesden, wheelwright. (*Courtesy of Folkestone Public Library*)
3   *Right* Dad, about 1954

old photograph, on tinplate, of the visit of a steam saw outfit to the yard; a rough guess is that this would date at about 1900. It shows two members of the family with some other workers.

Dad was born in 1879. He came to the shop as an apprentice to Frederick Maplesden, at the age of twelve. He married Mr Maplesden's daughter, Alice, in 1911 and later continued the concern under his own name. He volunteered for the Army during World War I, and, as he was then already in his thirties, the experience split his whole life into 'before the Great War' and 'after the Great War'. Later he would often talk about his war experiences, but hardly ever wanted to discuss wheelwrighting matters. But he was a craftsman through and through, even if he did find it a bore to talk 'shop'. He would often laughingly refer to himself and anyone else working in the shop as 'wood spoilers'. Usually he would discontinue whatever work he was doing if anyone called into the shop, and this was probably common practice, as most woodworking jobs require full concentration in order to prevent silly mistakes or minor accidents.

The Second War left Dad at work on his own, as Bert was away in the Army. During this wartime period the undertaking side of the work was given up. After Bert was demobbed, he gradually took over the running of the work as Dad never became acclimatized to the increase of red tape. However, Dad accompanied Bert on all local jobs, and even went pillion on Bert's motor cycle to outlying farm jobs. A minor health upset when he was eighty-four caused him to go into semi-retirement, but he continued to do various things about the shop. When his interest in the shop finally faded, he continued to care for his garden, until, just a fortnight before he died, he carefully put away his gardening tools for the last time. He passed away on 9 April 1973 at the age of ninety-three.

Much of Bert's experience within his family craft suggests an almost intact picture of the former place held by the woodcraft practitioners within a village community. Many of his customers are sons and grandsons of those who used to come to his father and grandfather for work to be done. Some jobs today are quite large enough for Bert to tackle singlehanded, whilst others are those little things for which any handyman would give up half an hour in order to help out a neighbour.

Bert can remember that he had very few toys as such when he was small, and various items around the place were adapted for use as alternatives. One example was an old roller-scotch with its two chains, and it was fun to dash about the garden pulling the little roller behind. Other toys were scraps of wood from the shop, small square, round and triangular pieces which were useful as building bricks. Before childhood days were over he became part of the work force of the place. Whilst still a schoolboy he would often be required to take a wooden wheel on his way to school and leave it at Mr Goldup the village blacksmith's shop for tyring, and collect it again on the way home. Bringing one home was the worst part, for it had to be rolled up Church Hill, and Bert would have his work cut out with a large wheel and have to weave a zigzag course to make any progress.

4   The Wheelwrights Arms, Matfield. One of a set of drawings on the theme
'trades and inns' by Ted Hayward of Ashford. The border of this example includes
tools of the wheelwright's craft, and the figures are from old photographs of
Bert's father

School-leaving age was fourteen for Bert. There was always plenty of hard
work to be done, and, as a matter of course, there were no wages then for the
son of a craftsman. Dad said Bert had food and clothes and a roof over his head;
that was what many dads of the time must have told their sons. There was nothing
arguable about it, for there was little enough cash to meet such giddy commitments as pocket money. Money was not considered a polite subject for talk
anyway, especially by Dad, who would willingly have gone through life free of
the need to have anything to do with it at all.

Bert's work now seems to remain in doing various farm and household
carpentry, decorating and repairs for local people. Always his family have been
involved in the village tradition of supplying services to people nearby, so that
the newer practice of using wheelwrighting skills in renovating horse-drawn
vehicles for a wider clientele holds no particular appeal for him. He loves the

creative work of wheelwrighting, and is pleased to see that there is some revival of interest in it, but there is little demand in the immediate locality for this type of work. It is also difficult to obtain the seasoned wood needed for it. However, Bert maintains his interest by occasionally making demonstration wheels so that craft details can be recorded. He has met enthusiasts in the field of model-making, and is inspired by them to regard the hobby as a good way of recording, when he retires, the design of carts and waggons once made in his shop.

CHAPTER 2

Timber

INTERMINGLED with the story of any country wheelwright's place is that of the local woodlands. In the case of the Kingsnorth shop a large part of the woodlands of the village was in the estate held by the Worshipful Company of Haberdashers for many years, as noted in the following quotation from the sale catalogue of 1951 when the lands were put up for sale by auction:

> On Park Farm is the site of the original Manor of Kingsnorth mentioned by the Kentish topographer – Hasted, who traces its history from the time of John de Kingsnorthe 'who lived here about the latter end of King Edward I . . . Alexander Andrews, executor and devisee of William Andrews in 1690 conveyed this manor with the farm called the Park and other Lands in this parish he being enabled to do so by Act of Parliament to the Company of the Haberdashers of London as trustees for the support of the Hospital at Hoxton commonly called Askes Hospital'.

The names of the local woodlands of the estate included: Stumble Wood, Park Wood, Cutler's Wood, Buttesland Wood, Calves Wood, Sticket Wood, Isaac Wood. It seems practically a certainty that some timber from these woods was bought at the old timber sales as supplies for the wheelwright's shop. Perhaps some standing trees were also bought; the old barking irons for taking bark from newly felled oak trees still hang in the shop.

One reminder of the busy local timber scenes of former days is in the name of Sawlodge Corner which is on the main road leading from Kingsnorth to Ashford. To most people today this may mean nothing more than a tricky bend for the unwary motorist – as quite a few can testify – but to a lifelong resident of the village it brings reminders of long-past days when some of the timber from the Haberdashers' estate was converted there. It is said that there was also an estate maintenance building on the Sawlodge site.

Not long after the 1951 sale two of the woodland areas were cleared for agricultural reasons. One of these was Cutler's Wood which was on the opposite side of the road from the wheelwright's shop. This immediately exposed the shop and its occupants to the relentless north winds, and the disappearance of this wood continues to be a matter of family commiseration.

Another bit of history of the local woodlands is to be found in the neighbouring village of Hamstreet. An area of woodland called the Hamstreet Woods National Nature Reserve has some trees which are said to be descendants of the mediaeval forest which once stretched from Winchester to Ashford. The great oak at the Wealden village of Headcorn in Kent is considered to be an actual tree of this former forest, and stands near the south porch of the church. The residents of Headcorn carefully preserve this tree; it continues to thrive despite the fact that it has now become completely hollow, and the branches have to be propped up.

How would the wheelwright go about making the best choice of timber for his special needs? What would be the very first consideration on stopping to examine a likely tree? He would almost automatically find out where the first bough or scar occurred, for if it was fairly high it would mean a good amount of unknotted wood from the trunk for the more important sections of a waggon – or even some nice planks for coffin boards!

Perhaps his second study would be to see that there was no evidence of nails or wire having been applied at some point in its history, for this not only caused distortion of grain, but also told of hidden metal remnants to spoil the saws which would later convert the timber. Hedgerow trees were the most likely offenders for this, where a bit of rough fencing might have been done.

With these two considerations out of the way, a general study of the size, shape and condition helped towards a decision. The wheelwright also often bought peculiarly shaped trees, as they would possibly yield the curved pieces needed in some parts of vehicle construction. Apart from its physical appearance, the wheelwright would note the type of ground in which the tree had grown. Some soils or positions could affect the nature of the wood. In fact some areas might produce a tree which was outwardly quite impressive, but when it was finally converted there would be disappointment – perhaps even a core of useless consistency. These little local geographical secrets were amongst the likely ones to be passed from father to son, and were worth taking heed of. It was also wise to note that there was no impediment to prevent cartage of the tree from its site.

In the case of the woodland trees, some would be available for sale from a wood about every thirteen years, as that is the time needed for the underwood to mature into useful, saleable condition. The woods were cared for by the wood reeves, who would maintain the ditches and hedges. They were expert at laying a hedge, an old skill no longer in much demand.

When a parcel of wood was ready to yield its harvest of usefulness, the woodmen were the first to arrive on the scene, their job being to clear the underwood so that the timbermen had room to fell the selected trees later on. The underwood produced many useful items and as the woodmen cleared it they were kept busy cutting bean poles and pea boughs. Spiles would be made if chestnut was amongst the underwood; also the large hop poles for hop gardens. Quite often poles would be suitable to cut out as clothes-line props. The twigs and sticks would be made up into the bundles known as faggots, and these were mainly sold for household firewood. Even the very finest fronds of wood twigs (known as the brushwood) were utilized for filling across ditches in the wood where the carters would later need a pathway for their carthorses and vehicles. Brushwood was also needed by farmers for use as footings for building hay and corn stacks. Hazel twigs could be made into a 'witches' broom' type of appliance for cleaning the mud away from boots before taking them off.

With the underwood cleared the timbermen would be able to get on with their heavy and skilled task of felling the big trees. Axes, saws, wedges, ropes and hard work would be the ingredients for this job. When the trees were felled they would need to be trimmed of the branches, and these would then be cut into cordwood. Sometimes a branch was tripartite and it could therefore be used to make a useful three-legged chopping block to sell for sixpence or a shilling to a householder for chopping up faggots, and so formed a useful 'perk' for the timbermen. Cordwood itself was usually sawn into logs and sold for household fuel.

If oak was felled in spring, then the bark would be removed as neat strips and sold to the tanneries by the cord for the tanning of leather. At other times of the year the oak bark would not 'run' (peel away). Apart from the oak bark being a

5   *Left* Naturally formed chopping block, a tripartite branch, was sold direct to country dwellers for a few pence
6   *Right* Flawing (removing) the bark with barking tool or spud

7   Stacking bark to dry before it was carted to the local tanneries

saleable commodity which helped to pay for the tree-felling work, it was as well to get the bark off the tree trunk anyway, as the wood then seasoned more satisfactorily than if it was left on. A cord of wood was measured by knocking four stakes of wood into the ground at pre-determined measurements and the area within these stakes was filled to the top of the stakes which were also to a certain measurement of height.

As the timbermen finished their work, so the carters would come with their horses and tugs to cart the tree trunks to a place where there was a sawpit, or in later times to a sawmill. The carters had knowledge and skills of simple leverage methods together with ropes, chains and horsepower whereby they got their vehicles loaded and unloaded.

Once the various people concerned in the work had all left the wood, the wood reeve would again see to his domain, clearing the brushwood from the tracks and repairing the hedges or fences where exits had been made for hauling away the timber.

When a useful number of trees was safely at the wheelwright's yard, the sawyers would be asked to visit and saw them into planks and pieces. Before the steam-driven saws came into being, this was done by two sawyers at the sawpit. The sawyers were skilled men, despite the dreary nature of their work.

8   Timber loading   9   Timber hauling

Each trunk had to be manoeuvred into position over the pit, and this was an art in itself, using various levers and iron grips. When a trunk was on the pit the guide lines for sawing were marked out with chalked twine sprung against it. A line and plumb was hung over to make lines on the end of the trunk; the trunk was then turned over and matching lines made on the underside. The trunk could then be settled over the pit for the actual sawing work, and iron timber dogs knocked into both the trunk and the beams to keep everything steady.

In the sides of the pit were little niches for oil cans and rags, also, hopefully, for a bottle of cold tea. With everything set up, and a well-sharpened saw, the work could begin. The top sawyer stood on the trunk, and was also the senior worker. The bottom sawyer was subjected to the discomforts of sawdust showering onto him; the saw actually cut on the downward pull, thus needing more power from him than from his partner. (It used to be said that a growing lad should not work in the sawpit, for there was a tendency to become round-shouldered as a result.) The pit saw would have a detachable handle at its lower end, so that the saw could conveniently be lifted out whenever necessary.

As the work proceeded the master of the yard would observe progress and give any special instructions according to his assessments of the possibilities suggested by each tree, and the qualities it showed as it was sawn.

The absolute monotony of sawing at the pit is difficult to imagine. The staff of a wheelwright's place were usually too busy with their normal work to engage on

10 Pit sawing

taking a turn at pit sawing, and they were probably only too glad that the sawyers were called in to cope with that unpopular job.

The steam-sawing era brought special excitements of its own. A full outfit would travel around from yard to yard. Quite a paraphernalia followed in the wake of these steam monsters: probably a living van, also a watercart, and plenty of coal either waiting at the place or brought in another trailer. There would be the driver and the chief sawyer, not to mention some casual labour. Even with such mechanical aid, the sawyer had a busy time seeing that the timber was handled to best advantage; also the saws would need his expert attention in being sharpened and set.

The team who came with the steam-driven saw would seem to have better living conditions, with the living van being part of the set-up. Their predecessors would usually sleep 'rough' at the scene of their work, perhaps two to four weeks being spent at one place, it usually being too much distance to walk back to their homes at night. Woodmen and timbermen were also amongst the travelling workmen who endured makeshift conditions like that, according to where their work happened to take them. Once at the scene they worked very long hours as a matter of course. Stories of grumpy sawyers going off to the local pub when things were not aright (e.g. sudden blunting of the saw against nail or wire in the wood) must have been all too true, as the general conditions of the job would be enough to send anyone to such refuge and consolation. Travelling workmen's diet, too, would be pretty makeshift. Bread, cheese, beer, tea, eggs, perhaps. One elderly man who had once been a sawyer with a steam outfit described how some straying chicken had taken the bacon out of the frypan on their camp fire, but one of the men took chase and carefully retrieved the precious and now rather grubby victuals.

The stacking of sawn timber for seasoning was closely supervised by the master, for there were important points about this which could make or mar the final condition of the wood. It would have to lie in a straight, flat position, and the pieces be built up with little segments of wood placed between to allow air to circulate around every plank or piece. A lean-to roof would be the thing, thus keeping the rain off, but allowing plenty of air.

Elm logs were an important consideration to the wheelwright, as these were for the naves of wheels; there were very few short cuts in the seasoning of these. The rule of at least a year's seasoning for every inch of thickness applied to these thick logs just as much as to a one-inch thick plank, so that a log of over twelve inches diameter would be in the seasoning process for a long time. There were one or two tricks to help speed up the process, although many craftsmen were not too keen about them. The craftsmen always knew, almost as if by instinct, when a particular piece of wood was fit to use.

Not all of the wheelwright's timber had to be sawn. Wheel spokes would be fashioned from cleft heart of oak. Cleaving was yet another way of converting

11　Elm logs for naves. (*Courtesy of the Weald and Downland Open Air Museum*)
12 and 13　*Right* These two photographs show the cleaving of a tree trunk, using wedges. Iron wedges were often used, but wooden ones were used whenever possible as they minimize damage to the fibres of the cleft wood

timber, and had to be done to spring-felled trees because the sap content then aided this work. The woodmen drove wedges (often of wood) into the trunk and then blows with a large mallet type of tool, called a beetle, would split the wood along the grain. Cleaving preserved all the strength of the longitudinal grain and so was the natural choice for making spokes; old fashioned gates were also often made of cleft oak. Some other woodland crafts also depended on supplies of cleft wood.

The supplies of seasoned timber would be slowly rotational, so that the craftsman might never actually himself work on the trees he had originally chosen, but his successors would reap the benefit of his choice in years to come. Elm, oak, ash and beech were the main woods needed for the country workshop. In more recent times all timber was bought from the timber merchant, and foreign woods have been added to the lists – many of which are extremely useful to the carpenter and joiner, although the wheelwright himself is rather at a disadvantage without the well-seasoned English grown hardwoods which were once so plentiful.

CHAPTER 3

Waggons and Carts

At the Kingsnorth shop the waggon building is now only a memory to Bert. He was about seventeen when the last complete new waggon was sent out, although some waggon repairs have been done since then, and quite a few new carts made.

A horse-drawn waggon is a load-carrying vehicle which has four wheels, whilst a cart has only two wheels.

Regional differences in waggon design have always existed. In earlier times, with so little intercommunication between villages, these were often very marked, but eventually the factory-produced vehicles of the nineteenth century tended to influence the village work, and the 'boat' and 'barge' waggon designs became apparent. Barge waggons have deep, box-like bodies, whilst the sides of boat waggons splay out into a more shallow-looking body. A 'bow' waggon is of the older school, and has graceful curves along the top of the sides for load clearance over the wheels. The Oxfordshire waggon is an example of this design; to see such a vehicle actually being drawn by a well-groomed horse gives insight as to why there is much revival of interest in both vehicles and horses.

The theme of regional waggon design has considerable appeal to the enthusiast, but most would probably agree that, even within the regions, each hand-built waggon is individual in some way or another. The older generations of wheelwrights could usually tell in which of the neighbouring shops a vehicle had been made, just by noting little differences in the handiwork.

One major part of waggon design which produces variations is the way the extent of the front wheel lock is accommodated. Some waggons have very little lock and may, perhaps, just have a place cut into each side of the vehicle body to allow clearance when turning. Other waggons have rather more lock, and need an appropriate allowance incorporated in the design. Thus, for example, the Kent or Sussex waggon has a waisted part at the front portion of the vehicle body.

The best and thickest timber of a waggon goes into the parts underneath the body, for there lies the strength and durability of a vehicle. A carefully thought-out framework, the undercarriage or hindcarriage, carries the back axle and supports the body, whilst the forecarriage takes the front axle and turning mechanism. The body itself has another strong under-framing and rests upon

14 Oxfordshire
waggon

intermediate layers of strong cross members often called the bolsters and pillows. Incorporated in the hindcarriage is a long central member, running fore and aft, usually called the carriage pole, and this is bolted at a point where it acts as a link between hind and forecarriage. The bolt usually goes through the floor of the body, the bolster, the pole and the forecarriage, thus it can be seen that this is a vital transmission point for the pull of the horse. The bolt is seated loosely through these parts which must either swivel or remain *in situ* as the forecarriage moves with each turn of the front wheels.

    The shafts of a waggon are detachable, as also, of course, are the wheels. Various devices which help the vehicle to take bulky loads, such as hay, can be added when needed, and usually consist of racks or upright corner poles. Some waggons can even be open-sided when needed, e.g. the Kent hop or pole waggon, which is simple in design but versatile in the uses it is designed for. Provision is usually made for rope tying and tightening for the securing of loads, by means of iron fittings at the rear of the body. Another accessory is the roller-scotch, a small iron-bound wooden roller which is draped with chains near the rear of a wheel when needed, and acts as a safety stop should it happen that the vehicle could run backwards down an incline. There is also an iron skid pan which is placed, when

GLAMORGAN WAGGON

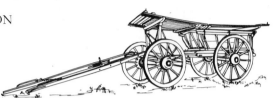

HERMAPHRODITE

EAST-ANGLIAN WAGGON

HEREFORD WAGGON

BUCKINGHAMSHIRE BARGE WAGGON

ESSEX PLANK-SIDED WAGGON

HOP WAGGON

15 These examples demonstrate the wide differences occurring in waggon design. (Drawings by John Thompson, from recent illustrated catalogues of his plans for model-making)

16 Carriage pole of a waggon under the cross members near its link with the forecarriage. Photograph of derelict waggon taken by model-making enthusiast Richard Walker as reference material in the course of making scale model

17 Cast iron skid pan. Placed under a wheel to hold vehicle back on a forward incline. (*Courtesy of John Ferridge*)

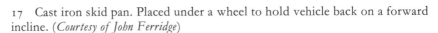

needed, under a wheel to help hold the vehicle back on a forward incline. A tie-chain is a further means of anchoring a wheel. There can also be the dog stick fitted to some waggons; this digs into the ground should the vehicle start to run back.

Another characteristic of the regional waggon is the colour scheme adopted by different localities or individual waggon builders, although there can always be surprise exceptions within a region. Kent waggons were often in ochre, with red undercarriage, wheels and shafts, whilst neighbouring Sussex favoured blue with red.

The size of a waggon is significant, and usually referred to as one-horse, two-horse, three-horse, etc. Many farm waggons were designed so that the extra horses were added by means of linking with chains in single line, but some had double shafts with two horses abreast. The harness design varied accordingly.

Whatever the individual or local design, each waggon was built with unerring craftsmanship. George Sturt described them as being almost like living organisms, as they had become so closely adapted in design through the ages to their environment. They certainly represent a quality of carpentry which can never be excelled. To fashion a fairly complex vehicle almost wholly from wood seems enough of a task, and yet, with proper use and care, one of those hand-made waggons would last over a hundred years. Another point is that ample supplies

18 Two-horse team and waggon

of the right kind of wood were available to those village craftsmen. Nowadays, the cost of searching for such materials would be disproportionate to the price of a waggon. The time spent in making a waggon, if paid for at the proper rate, would be another obstacle nowadays. In former days the matter of time was not really allowed for in the cost of a vehicle, and to note that one of Bert's ancestors charged £6 for a new light waggon and the painting of it in 1871 makes strange reading, remembering that it took very many hours to build such a vehicle.

One characteristic of waggon- and cart-building is that the joints are nearly all tapered and bevelled, and when they are driven together during assembly they become extremely tight. A wheelwright prides himself on these joints. However, each new vehicle is assembled twice. The first time is a sort of test to see if everything fits well. If found to be satisfactory the vehicle is almost fully taken apart and the separate parts chamfered with a spoke shave and smoothing plane. This is done primarily to remove weight, but it also gives a neat decoration. No glue is used in the final assembly; the old-fashioned glue was unsuitable, anyway, and the aim was to produce a properly jointed structure able to withstand the stresses and strains of load-carrying over uneven ground. Final assembly involves drawpinning the main joints. Drawpinning can only be done where there is a shouldered tenon. The holes to take the wooden dowel pin are bored out in the normal way

19   South Midlands waggon, at Wye College Agricultural Museum, Brook, near Ashford, Kent, which is open on Wednesday afternoons in the summer. (*Courtesy of the Museum*)

FARM TIP CART

DUNG CART

WELSH LONG CART

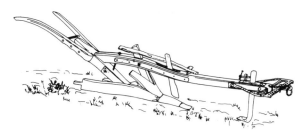

TURNWREST PLOUGH

TIMBER BOBS

20   Three types of cart, a plough and timber bobs. (Drawings by John
Thompson, from recent catalogues of his plans for model-making)

in the morticed part of the joint, but the hole in the tenon tongue must be out of line and nearer the shoulder. This will then mean that the tapered dowel pin will have to be hammered with some force to go through both the normally placed dowel holes and the off-centre one in the tenon. Once the pin is home, the effect is to draw the tenon shoulder up tightly against the morticed section. Such a pin taken from an old gate or waggon will show that a marked kink has developed over the years.

The difficulties and shortages of the Second War years meant that sometimes the shafts of old waggons were removed and replaced with tractor drawbars. Though so sturdily built, the waggons were never meant other than for horse-drawn use. The speed and power of a tractor would wrench the joints too much, and the waggons had no suitable springing either.

As late as the 1950's it was possible to buy an old waggon at an auction sale for about a pound, and nothing was thought of breaking one up for firewood, there being, as yet, no collectors' value on them. Farmers tipped them into ponds when these were being filled in, or set them alight to get the old broken or disused things out of the way. Even if a farmer tried to hang on to such vehicles, they would generally have to stand out in the open as covered space is always at a premium in farming. Despite everything, quite a few vehicles have survived, having either been well preserved or lovingly restored. It is possible to view waggon and cart exhibits at a number of public museums, whilst private collectors often generously allow visitors.

The hobby of model-making is another means of contact. Plans are produced by enthusiasts from on-the-spot measuring and drawing of actual vehicles, and a scale model of an authentic design can thus be made from either one's own plans or those purchased from a specialist. The woodworking and model magazines often carry advertisements for such plans, which are also ideal for study purposes, or even as wall pictures.

The waggons are so interesting that it might be easy to overlook the carts. However, the wheelwrights could not afford to do this; the carts were much too useful to the farmer, and often likely to be on order. Cart design also varied from place to place. Some ingenious all-purpose carts were designed when reasons of economy caused the farmer to want a light, adaptable vehicle needing only one horse. The Scotch cart, especially, was a fairly universal favourite. Dung carts with their inevitable tipping mechanism were present on practically every farm.

In addition to carts and waggons, there were other kindred vehicles. The hermaphrodite was a combination of both cart and waggon, being basically a cart which had an extra pair of wheels to add to the front part to make it into a four-wheeled vehicle when there were bulky loads such as hay and corn sheaves to carry. Timber-hauling vehicles were also likely to be built in country shops, or even in the estate shop of a large land owner. Some village shops built the later market vans, milk floats and other light vehicles, but, in a way, the study of these and the coachbuilt class does seem to be in a field of its own. The older, heavy, agricultural vehicles seem to be the essence of things, symbolizing the work of the country craftsman.

It is a pleasant pastime to sit in a warm home of today and read and think about the various horse-drawn vehicles of yesterday, or to set off in a modern car on good, hard roads and perhaps visit a museum or two to examine some waggons, carts and carriages. However, the following account from *Hasted's History of Kent*, 1798 acts as a reminder that things were not always too good for those actually involved. The description refers to High Halden, a village between Tenterden and Ashford, and is from a piece of *Hasted's* quoted in *Thomson's 1918 Almanac and Directory (Tenterden)* – price three halfpence:

'The soil is a deep stiff clay. The turnpike road from Tenterden to Bethersden and Ashford, leads through it, which, as well as the rest of the roads throughout it are hardly passable after any rain, being so miry, that the travellers horse frequently plunges through them up to the girths of the saddle; and the waggons sinking so deep in the ruts, as to slide along on the nave of the wheels and axle of them. The roads are all of great breadth, from fifty to sixty feet and more, with a breadth of green swerd on each side; the hedges being filled with oak trees, whose branches hang over to a considerable extent and render the surface near them damp, and the prospect always gloomy. In some few of the principal roads, as from Tenterden hither, there is a stone causeway about three feet wide for the accommodation of horse and foot passengers; but there is none further on till near Bethersden, to the great distress of travellers. When these roads become tolerably dry in summer, they are ploughed up and laid in a half circle to dry, the only amendment they ever have. In extreme dry weather in summer, they become exceedingly hard, and by traffic so smooth as to seem glazed like a potter's vessel, though a single hour's rain renders them so slippery, as to be very dangerous to travellers.'

21   The shop in 1905

CHAPTER 4

The Shop and Yard

A CASUAL VISITOR to the Kingsnorth shop today would probably not notice anything of outstanding interest, just an old weather-boarded building containing some shabby-looking tools and equipment. This would be the natural reaction, of course, as it sums up the actuality. It is the history and associations which really count, and Bert's own memories add a further vital dimension. The tools themselves are worn to special shapes where they have been grasped and used by generations of craftsmen; perhaps there is a strengthened bond with the past in the fact that the tools are still in the same site where they have actually been used. Removal to a museum would sever this special link, although it is really the continued presence of a craftsman which breathes life into any such work place.

There was almost certainly a happiness and satisfaction in working at this rural craft which overcame the rather spartan conditions. The ability of the former workers to be content with their lot seems to have left a sense of tranquillity. It now seems a mercy and a reprieve that Dad was not inclined to keep up with the times for he has thereby preserved something of an old country way of life for at least a little while longer in a world which craves speed and yet envies some lost element which existed in the days of the hand craftsmen.

Some time around the middle of the last century the Maplesdens moved shop from nearby Stumble Lane to the present site. They built a new workshop for themselves, and this was unusual as village crafts often had to be carried out in various makeshift buildings which happened to be available. Even a sawpit was dug out at the new premises, and smartly lined with bricks, although the travelling steam-driven saws must soon have come into vogue. However, the sawpit continued to be handy for any sawing jobs which occurred between the visits of the steam-saw. Bert can recall having sawn at the pit with Dad – probably to convert a tree trunk to suitable sizes which could then be managed with the circular saw. (The pit has been filled in for some years now, but Bert often considers excavating it in order to reconstruct the sawpit scene.)

Access from the road leads straight into a yard, where there would have once been quite a few horse-drawn vehicles in for repair, or waiting for their owners to collect them. One of the two main buildings has tall sliding doors. This building is a relic of the beginning of the motor vehicle era when Dad had visions of orders for building numbers of lorry and bus bodies onto ex-works chassis. There turned out to be little demand locally for such work, and the family has never gone in for advertising, so it ended up with there only being about three such orders ever being placed before mass-production methods displaced the individually-built product. One of these was a carrier's type of vehicle which also converted into a bus as required, e.g. for childrens' outings. Another vehicle was a bus, and quite recently the author and Bert met a man who remembered being its driver when it plied a route from Bilsington to Ashford and also from Ashford to Hythe. The site of the former sawpit happens to be in this building.

Again out in the yard, one has to imagine the large stocks of timber which once would have been under lean-to roofs for the purpose of seasoning. Bert's grandfather also kept some timber stock in Stumble Lane. Sometimes Dad would spend half a day searching these stocks for just the right piece of wood for a job which had turned up.

Now to the older main building, which is the wheelwright's shop. This too, has double doors, though not so tall. Swinging them open to let in some light, the ancient wheelstool always seems to be just inside, as it still acts as a most useful support for many carpentry jobs. The work benches are against the walls, and this is always the case in a wheelwright's shop, for the main central space of such a shop needs to be clear for a vehicle to stand during its making or repair. In a joinery shop, on the other hand, the benches can quite conveniently be free standing.

The tools are within handy reach in their racks on the walls, and all kinds of other little nooks and crannies seem to occur for the storage of tools. Perhaps little recesses made just under the bench, or parts of the woodwork of the wall suggest yet more possibilities. The awl gets pushed into a part of this woodwork, and so is always at hand. There need to be plenty of nests of miniature drawers to hold such things as nails, screws, bolts, washers and staples. The immediate declaration that this is a wheelwright's shop is made by the many felloe patterns which hang above the bench. Trestles and various other supports for wheel and general work are dotted about. Years ago there was the 'great wheel' which was turned by hand to supply power for the wheelwright's lathe. The outer circumference of this wooden wheel acted as a flywheel to gain momentum and force as it was turned. At present there is electric power for an old lathe, the old bandsaw, the grindstone, and the circular saw which was bought from Mr Heathfield on the closing of his Godinton Road works. The old chopping block cannot be overlooked – for that is another symbol of any wheelwright's place.

A former feature was the shoeing hole for straking just inside the double doors, but this has been filled in as the wooden cover became a nuisance once the pit was not needed.

Some timber can be stored on the beams, and access is assisted by a little hatch door over the main doors. Timber used to be everywhere in the old days, but ever-increasing prices do not now permit the carrying of much stock.

22 Just one view in the paint shop of the encrustations of paint where
generations of workers have cleaned brushes off at the end of each day's work

The paint shop adjoins, but it was a later addition, as proved by an old yellowed
photograph which does not show the paint shop. Even so, the paint shop looks
quite ancient, and features the museum-class relic of encrustations of paint on the
walls and doors where countless paint brushes have been cleaned off at the end
of a day's work. There is also a tiny nest of drawers in which each drawer has
traces of coloured powdered pigment which would have been used in the mixing
of paints – blue, prussian blue, red, ochre and black. Earlier relics of a wheel-

wright's shop would have been the mullstone and muller for pounding solid pigment into powder form for paint-making.

The atmosphere of antiquity is furthered by the uneven earthen floor, which, after years of wear has become impacted nearly to the hardness of concrete. A piece of waste iron shows here and there embedded in the earth, and a few stones and bricks also show. The earth has a faintly pleasant air as it blends with the scent of wood shavings. The wheelwright likes an earthen floor, as it means less likelihood of the edge of a tool being blunted if it is accidentally dropped, as also would a layer of wood shavings or sawdust. Dad, however, had a passion for having a really deep layer of shavings. This was sometimes a nuisance for if anyone dropped a tool or small object it would be like looking for a needle in a haystack to try and retrieve it. Fred Smith, another of his apprentices who later stayed on at the shop, used to be heartily glad if Dad went out; and as soon as he was safely out of the way would have a grand sweep up and get rid of a lot of the accumulation. Even when Bert came home on leave during the War, one of the first jobs he did would be to sweep the shop floor, amid protests and grumbles from Dad.

Each of the windows is different, and glazed with all kinds of odd pieces of glass. They would have been old windows removed in the course of various house repairs. This economical use of such materials as might have been available to the family is reflected in the roofing, for one side of the shop is done with slates, whilst the other side has Kent peg tiles. The building itself is fashioned from timber and clad with weatherboard.

CHAPTER 5

Wheel Work

THERE ARE aspects of wheelwrighting which involve the coachbuilding class of work. Also, a wide range of skilfully designed machines for wheelmaking came into use towards the end of the nineteenth century – largely, it would seem, because of the American influence. The author has seen examples of such machines which are in use to this day.

Whilst being aware that there were, and still are, these other most necessary approaches to wheelwrighting, this book is mainly concerned with old country methods for hand-made wheels for horse-drawn agricultural vehicles.

'Everything is worked from the centre.' That is the wheelwright's motto for wheelmaking. Therefore, in a description of stages of this work, the central nave is the first consideration. The country wheelwright nearly always uses elm for this vital part; the reason being that this wood does not split, owing to its having a very curly and tough grain formation.

The initial log is trimmed with an axe, and then turned up on the wheelwright's lathe. The wheelwright gets the shape of the first nave of a pair without much measuring, and to make an identical nave he only has to use a few caliper measurements from the original at the final stages of turning. Nave design is usually bull-nosed for farm waggons; naves for lighter vehicles are more likely to be of carriage pattern. Two light marks about half an inch apart are scribed onto the nave whilst still in the lathe to show the morticing line. Iron nave hoops are fitted by the blacksmith before the next stage. These are the iron bands, fitted over the front and back of the wooden nave, which give safety and strength to the life of a wheel. One at a time is driven on whilst red hot and the nave is then carefully dipped in water to shrink it on. Small iron pegs are next driven in to secure it.

The next thing is to mark the nave with dots to show where the mortices to take the spokes are to be cut. The dividers are used, and the wheelwright develops a neat precision in gauging accurately. Always an even number of spokes is used. Holes are cut at these mortice positions with a brace and bit, and then the mortices are chiselled out. The special chisel used for the corners is the bruzz or buzz which has a long V-shaped blade. Things are complex, even at this stage, for it

may be that the wheel is to be dished, by means of inserting the spokes at an angle, and the mortices must be cut accordingly, and gauged by holding a straight-edge in the mortice and checking with the pointer on the spoke set.

During this stage of wheelmaking the work needs to be held fast on a suitable wooden horse, and provision is also needed to pivot the spoke set from the centre of the nave as required.

The spokes are next made, with oval section, the thicker part of the section for the inner side of the wheel. The drawknife and spoke shave are used for this general shaping. The spoke tenons to fit into the nave mortices are cut with the handsaw and the correct tapering for the joint must be effected. The outer ends of the spokes are longer than final requirement, to allow for wastage caused by damage inflicted by the sledgehammer in the next stage of work. In the country shop the spokes are invariably made of cleft heart of oak.

The spokes are now driven into the nave with a sledgehammer, and the spoke set gauge is frequently referred to in order to check that each spoke is being driven in at the correct angle as determined by the amount of dishing required. The mortices in the nave would have been cut to the lesser proportion of the tapering tenon, so the spokes have to be driven in with some force. Bert remembers that a bucket of water would be kept handy so as to dip the tenons into this, the water being deemed to act as a lubricant.

When all the spokes are driven in, the outer ends of the spokes can then be

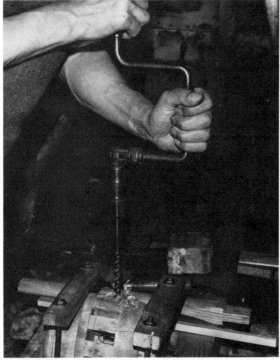

23   Trimming elm log with axe before turning
up the nave

24   Turning up elm log to make a nave

25   Brace and bit being used to bore holes prior
to mortice cutting with chisels

26   The special chisel with long V-shaped blade,
known as the bruzz or buzz, is used for cutting
the mortices in the nave

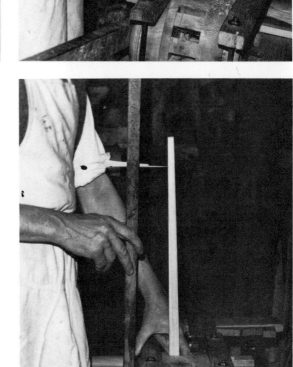

27   Using spoke set to check angle of mortice
which is formed with a slight angle for a dished
wheel. The straight-edge is held in the mortice
and read against the pointer on the spoke set

28   Shaping a spoke with spoke shave

29   Marking off shoulder for spoke tongue with try-square held against a gauged mark on the spoke set

30   Starting to form the spoke tongues with a chisel

31   Drawknife used both towards the worker and away from him in shaping spoke tongues

32 *Left* Spoke tongue gauge in use   33   *Above* Marking out felloes, using
wooden pattern. They will be cut out on bandsaw seen in picture, but in old
times the adze was used to shape them

marked off for the shoulders of the tongues which are to be made to fit into the
felloes which form the wooden rim of the wheel. The tongues are formed with
the tenon saw, chisel and then drawknife. For straked wheels the tongues would
be square, whilst a wheel with a continuous hoop tyre could have rounded or
square tongues.

The felloes are curved sections, each taking two of the spokes. Dowel joints
between the felloes will join them into a complete rim at final assembly. Felloes
are made of beech, ash or elm, and they are cut out from planks of suitable thickness by means of a bandsaw.

The wheel is next laid in a flat position on a suitable stool for assembly of the
felloes with the spokes. The spoke dog is used on a heavy wheel to pull each spoke
towards its matching place in the ring of felloes, and the dual operation of
assembling felloes into spokes and bringing the dowel joints together can be done.

34 Using the spoke dog to strain two spokes towards each other as the tongues are fitted into the holes in the felloe. The wheelwright has both hands free whilst he levers the shaft of the spoke dog with his shoulder

Tyres

With the woodwork of the wheel finished, the next stage is to apply the iron tyring. One method uses separate curved strips of iron (strakes), which are fitted around the wheel. These are applied red hot, and nailed on with strake nails. Each strake covers a wood joint in the rim of felloes. If more than one row of strakes is applied they are staggered to prevent two strake joints being in line. The wood joints of the felloes need to be gripped together whilst strakes are applied, and a large iron cramp called the samson is applied to do this. Strakes are fitted by the wheelwright, having been made by the blacksmith. Further notes on straking are at the end of this chapter.

The iron hoop tyres are fitted by the blacksmith, and it is unlikely that anyone but an experienced worker would be able to make a thorough success of this operation. It is too easy to end up with the tyre either too loose or too tight, either of which spells disaster. If too tight, the woodwork of the wheel can actually smash up at the time of tyring, whilst a loose tyre is virtually useless as the wood joints would be unduly strained in use and inclined to loosen in a very short time.

Tyre fitting can be either new work or done in the course of repair work. In new work a hoop is made up individually for each wheel, whilst in work following wood repairs the old tyre can usually be re-fitted. There can also be the need to re-fit a tyre simply because it has become loose, often because a vehicle has been exposed to alternating extremes of wet and dry conditions.

For every tyring job, however, the first move is to measure the perimeter of the wooden wheel. The measuring tool for this is the 'traveller' which is chalk marked and carefully run round the wooden rim from another chalk mark there. The number of revolutions is noted and a second chalk mark made for any remainder. Every time this sort of measuring is done, it is standard practice to check three

35 Iron strake

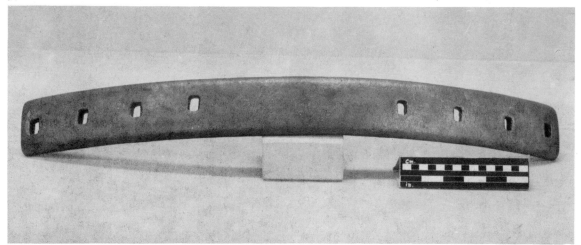

times. The blacksmith has also to make the right allowance for the amount of shrinkage which must occur at the finish of the job, and it is this consideration, drawn from years of experience, which makes or mars the work. The decided measurement is 'run out' with the traveller onto the flat iron bar and, after careful checks, the bar is cut and put through the rollers of an iron bender to form a circle. The ends are then welded together to form a complete hoop. For the re-fit of an old tyre, it is measured in the same way, and, if necessary, the tyre is altered by cutting and then shortening it, or lengthening it by adding a piece, before welding it together again. The old way of referring to this repair was usually 'to cut and shut' a tyre.

Whenever possible a number of tyres would be fitted at the same time, as a large fire of faggots and waste wood has to be lit for getting them red hot. The fire would usually be on open ground, but a busy place might have a furnace for this work. In summer it would probably be decided to make a really early start, so that some of the work was out of the way before the heat of the day added to the already warm conditions of the job.

Whilst the tyres are heating, the wooden wheel is clamped in position onto the iron wheel plate, which is also out-of-doors. When the tyres are red hot, the first one is pulled out with a long hook, and the smith and his helpers must move and work very quickly as a team at this stage. The helpers have large tyre tongs and lift up the tyre a little and drop it smartly to the ground to dislodge any clinging embers, and then quickly take it up again and drop it into position over the wheel. The tyre will look too small, but the blacksmith uses iron tyre dogs to lever the tyre over the wooden rim, and the helpers follow round with sledgehammer blows to fit the tyre completely. The hot tyre is burning the wood by now, and a flow of water is directed all round the work. The rapid shrinkage of the hot iron causes the already firm woodwork joints to be forced together very sharply indeed. The blacksmith ascertains that the work is satisfactory and the wheel can next be unclamped and taken to a nearby tank of water for total cooling. The wheel is then ready to be returned to the wheelwright's shop.

*   *   *

The final operation in making a new wheel is to fit the iron 'box' into the nave centre. The box is a cylinder which acts as a wheel bearing onto the iron axle arm of the vehicle. A hole has to be bored in the nave and gouged out with rounded chisels; then the box is driven in by sledgehammer blows, with a piece of wood placed over the box to prevent damage. The box itself is of cast iron and has fins on the outside which anchor it within the wood of the nave. It is slightly tapered in shape. When the box has been suitably fitted, small wooden wedges are driven in around it.

Older vehicles had completely wooden axles, and little iron plates were nailed on the axle arms to take the wear. The naves of these vehicles had different boxes;

36 Wheeltyring. Levering red hot iron tyre over the wooden rim with tyre dogs
whilst sledgehammer blows are applied to drive the tyre on completely.
Ardington, Wantage, Berkshire, 1959

these were in two separate sections within the nave centre. An ancient tool for boring the nave centre accurately for this type of box was called the boxing machine.

Finishing touches to the wheel are done with trimming tools and sandpaper, and the work primed and painted.

*   *   *

STRAKING

Each wheelwright's shop evolved its own special way of going about a particular job. This was natural as there could never be undue standardization in these older crafts. Some of the following notes on straking include a working method which Bert remembers following with Dad.

The strakes are cut, curved to shape and suitably punched with tapered nail holes by the blacksmith, who also makes the nails. A strake nail is tapering and wedge-like in shape with a prominent tapered head and chisel-like point. Some workers used to prepare the wooden felloes by boring holes ready to take these large, blunt nails, but Bert remembers that his father's practice was to file a sharp edge to the nails and use them directly into the wood. However, whichever method is used, the nail points tend to curl as they come up against the hard, well-seasoned wood, and this curled effect is useful in that the strake is held even more securely by these varied nail positions within the wood.

Whilst the strakes are heating in the fire, the wheel is placed vertically over the shoeing pit. It can be supported directly on the wooden frame of the pit, or from another higher frame, but it has to be possible to swing the wheel round so that a newly applied strake can be dipped into the water in the pit for cooling.

Between each felloe the dowelled wood joint has been left with a noticeable gap, and this gap must be closed before a strake is applied. The samson is the obvious choice for this, but Bert remembers that his father used wedges for part of this work, and applied the samson only for the last two strake applications to a wheel. Strakes are applied to opposite sections of the wheel rim in turn, so as to distribute the stresses as evenly as possible. The wedges are inserted into felloe joints according to order of working, their function being to close the gap in a neighbouring joint in this case; as soon as a strake is applied the wedges are removed, before another part of the rim is prepared.

A strake nail is tapped lightly into the rim, to act as a marker against which the red hot strake is to be laid. This is because the work has to be hurried at this stage, and there is no margin for adjustments. Once the strake is on the rim, the wheelwright must drive the nails in as quickly as possible. The nails are driven in with the chisel-like end placed across the grain of the wood. Once the strake is nailed on, the wheel can be turned to dip the hot work into the water. Certain strake nails are not fully driven home at first, as the protruding heads will be needed to act as gripholds for the application of the samson. Some descriptions have the wheel spokes also being used as gripholds, but Dad used the nail heads only. (Bert feels that there would be practical disadvantages in using the spokes; also, the samson itself has tapered edges which seem more suited to being placed under a nail head.)

The samson is a very weighty appliance, as the author well knows, having moved it around for photography purposes; it would seem a good thing to cut down on its use during straking work, and the method of using wedges was probably fairly universal.

CHAPTER 6

Tools of the Shop

Some of the special tools and equipment for wheelwrighting are primitive, and yet essential once the work of making a wheel is under way. This fact was well illustrated when Bert set out to make a demonstration wheel. He soon found out that he needed to make replicas of various wooden horses and frames which he and Dad had discarded years ago. The job is clumsy unless the wheel parts are properly supported during the making. Therefore, perhaps these supports should be discussed first.

When it is being worked on, the nave needs to be held fast, and for this purpose a strong frame with adjustable means to clamp the nave is used. The frame can be rested on a pair of trestles. Such a frame can also be more permanently incorporated over a wheel pit, and this is especially helpful when a large wheel is being made – especially at the stage where the spokes are driven into the nave with a sledge-hammer as the work is then at a convenient height for swinging the sledge. This frame is long, so that, as the spokes go into the nave, there is sufficient clearance on either side for them to be moved round.

The typical wheelstool supports a wheel for many of the stages, but chiefly it is useful when the spokes and felloes are being assembled. The wheelwright can lay the wheel on this stool and get well over the work and fix his shoulder against the spoke dog handle to lever a spoke towards its place in a felloe. Another horse is rather in the form of a tripod, and has an iron clamp to tighten the wheel down and stop it rotating as the spoke tongues are formed. A further support for a wheel is a stand with an iron spindle at the top to take the wheel centre. This position for the wheel makes it look like a large artificial flower, and is useful when painting as every part is accessible without the wet paint getting touched at all.

Tools for wheelmaking can conveniently be listed in the order in which they are likely to be used. The light axe is used for trimming the elm log in readiness for turning up on the lathe. In older times the nave would have been fashioned entirely by means of the axe. The lathes themselves vary according to the age of a shop, although the most typical would be those driven by means of turning the 'great wheel' by hand. (Many shops lasting into the present century would have passed through the later use of stationary engines followed by electrically-driven plant. In Bert's shop there is a blending of old and new; for example, the ancient bandsaw is now driven electrically, and yet the handle with which it could once be driven by hand is still in the shop, and it is amusing to place this into its slot and recall how unpopular a job it was to turn the bandsaw – that was really hard work. Dad once had a stationary engine which was very temperamental to start up, and when it refused, someone could get the job of turning the bandsaw by hand. When the engine was finally coaxed to start, no-one would shut it off during the remainder of that day for fear that it would not restart. Even at the mid-day mealtime it would be left running.)

To continue with the tools for wheelmaking. During the turning of the nave the calipers are used to measure and match. Dividers are used to mark the places around the nave for morticing. The brace and bit is used to bore holes in the mortice places to clear some of the wood away before chiselling begins. Chisels for morticing the nave include the all-important buzz or bruzz, with its long V-shaped blade which cuts well into the corners of the deep mortices. One feature of all the wheelwright's chisels is that they are designed to cope with very hard, well-seasoned wood, and the wooden handle is let into a funnel-shaped socket. A chisel for soft wood, on the contrary, often has the handle attached by a tang arising from the tool blade. The wooden mallet, of course, is used in conjunction with chiselling operations.

As the nave is laboriously morticed the wheelwright needs a guide to see that he is getting the correct angle to each mortice. This guide is given by using the spoke set. It is a very plain-looking lath of wood, like a stout yardstick, with some holes into which a whalebone pointer can be inserted where required. (Older wheelwrights recall that the whalebone was rescued from discarded corsetry. Bert has to make do with pieces of cane.) One end of the spoke set is anchored at the nave centre, and the free end with the pointer can be swivelled into position whenever the work is to be checked. The spoke set is also essential in the later stage of driving the spokes into the nave; also for marking off spoke tongue shoulders. Several old spoke sets are in the shop, one or two are riddled with woodworm holes, as well as by holes caused by the awl being used as a marker during use of the try-square when marking shoulders of spoke tongues.

The busy job of morticing leads to an equally busy time in fashioning the spokes. The drawknife and spoke shave are the tools for general shaping; there are also the tenons to be made with the saw and chisel. Some wheelwrights like to make up a frame to hold a spoke for the shaping work, the practice of bracing one end against the worker's chest not always being very comfortable, besides accounting for a lot of frayed clothing. Bert uses this method, and the seemingly useful framework idea never seems to have existed in this shop. An essential part of ancient crafts is in the individual way of working, and no one shop or family could possibly work in the identical ways of another.

In most of the spoke-shaping work the wheelwright has only his eye to go by, as there cannot be any definite gauge as to how a spoke should be shaped. The

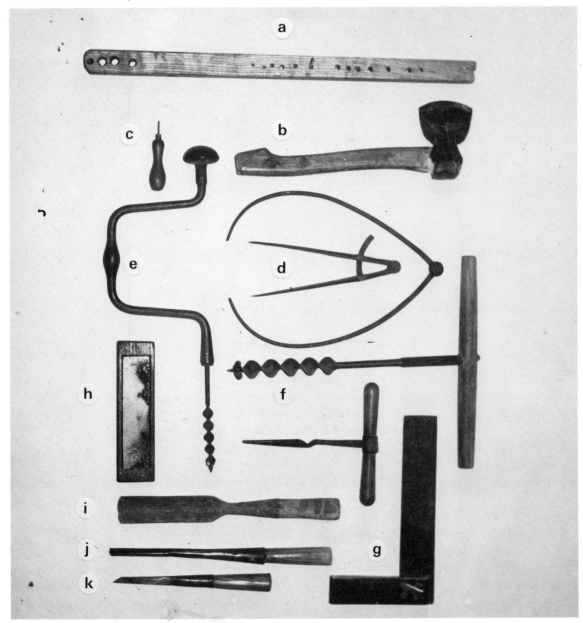

37   Some of the tools of the wheelwright's shop: (a) spoke set, (b) axe, (c) awl, (d) çalipers and dividers, (e) brace and bit, (f) auger, (g) try-square, (h) oil stone, (i) gouge chisel, (j) buzz, (k) morticing chisel, *Right* (l) drawknife, (m) spoke shave, (n) planes, (o) spoke tongue gauge, (p) adze, (q) adjustable circular plane, which can be set to either a concave or convex arc, (r) felloe pattern, (s) gauge for marking two dowel holes to ends of very large felloes, (t) traveller, (u) tyre dog made from an old strake, (v) samson, (w) tongs

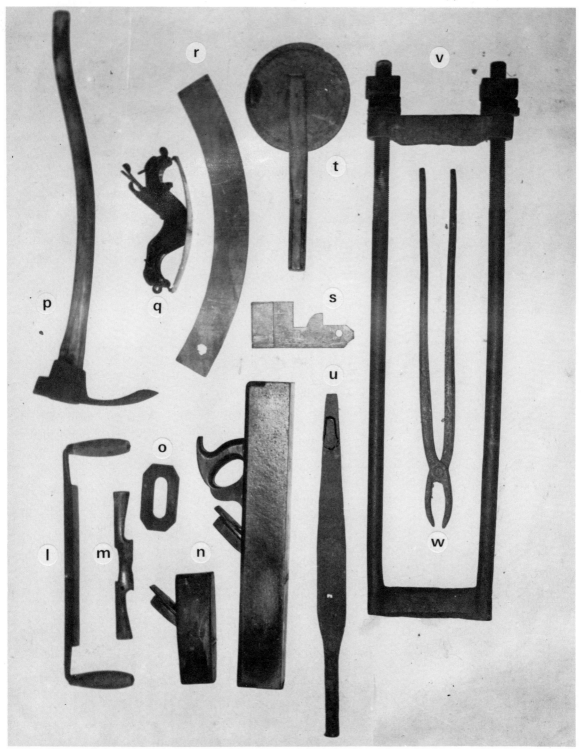

uniformity of the finished work goes a long way to show how correct learning of a hand craft in the early years of a person's life imprints itself upon his tactile abilities.

A neat-looking little shaping tool for spoke making is the spoke jarvis; it is a favourite item for collectors, but many wheelwrights do not seem to find a lot of use for it.

The felloes are cut out on the bandsaw. The dangerous-looking adze which had to be kept razor-sharp, used to be the tool for this job, and using it must have needed a very special skill. The adze has not been used for many years in this shop, of course, although Dad did put a long handle on one and used it for weeding the garden. All adzes are interesting, including the shipwright's adze, which has a little hammer-like protrusion on the non-cutting side. Chair bodgers also make good use of their special adzes.

A frame saw was another of the old tools for cutting out felloes, and often the sawyers would cut out some felloes with one during their visit to a yard, and these would be neatly stacked for seasoning with the other sawn timber.

The felloes are bored to receive the spoke tongues, and a dowel hole bored into the end of each. A large wheel needs two dowel holes in the felloe ends – special wooden gauges help to show the position for these. The brace and bit is again used for boring. Some older boring tools are the shell augers, and the amount of dust which has accumulated on the shop specimens shows that it is indeed a long time since they were last used.

For the dowels, some wooden pegs are first made with an axe at the chopping block, and then each peg is driven through the smaller side of a tapered hole in a flat piece of iron. This neatens the peg nicely and also gives an accurately sized dowel. These pieces of iron, with their varying-sized holes used for dowel making, can easily be overlooked as being merely scrap unless the wheelwright is there to explain things.

Assembling the felloes onto the spokes brings the spoke dog into use. This is about as symbolic a tool of the wheelwright's craft as any. When closely examined it is found to be just as primitive as many of the other tools, and also equally indispensable. It is like having a third, very strong hand available at a crucial point in wheelmaking. The spoke dog holds and levers a spoke so that it can be eased towards its place in the felloe. Because of the radial position of the bore holes in the felloe, the spoke tongues cannot be assembled into the felloe without first straining the spokes towards one another. It is necessary, however, for the spokes to be sufficiently long to have the amount of 'give' for straining them like this; short, thick spokes are unpopular because of the total resistance they offer.

The iron cramp known as the samson is a likely relic of any old wheelwrighting concern – especially as it could not be got rid of by burning as might have been the fate of many of the wooden things. It is used in the work of applying iron strakes to a wheel. At least two patterns of samson can be noted; one has a screw thread on each of its two legs, and nuts and washers push the cross piece against

38 Spoke dog

the work; the other has a centrally-placed screw which is tightened to do the same job.

Tongs for handling the hot strakes would also be found. Some other tools for coping with the ironwork on vehicles might be found in a shop if there had been a blacksmith on the staff. Sometimes the wheelwright himself might have a try at putting on a hoop tyre, but was not likely to be over-successful. More often than not he would have to be off to the blacksmith with crestfallen explanations, to get the ironwork done properly. The motto 'each man to his own trade' was a very true one in the case of old hand crafts.

The boxing machine is yet another tool of the older order, and helps to cut out the centre of the nave of a wheel which is for a wooden axled vehicle. The spiky legs brace against the nave whilst a handle is turned to rotate the cutting blade.

Waggon building itself uses many of the tools already described. In addition, there are some special long augers which are useful when pairing up holes in the opposite side of a vehicle, and also for reaching inaccessible parts. Wooden patterns for barrow parts and all kinds of patterns associated with cart and waggon design accumulate in a shop. These are cut out in thin wood by the wheel-wright, and parts of old things are saved as reference, too.

Even in a country shop which has never undertaken work in actually making the coachbuilt class of horse-drawn vehicles, there would be need for various maintenance tools to cope with any such vehicle which might need attention. There is ample evidence of this in Bert's shop. Special spanners to undo oil caps, lock nuts, and nuts for removing a wheel; jacks to support a vehicle whilst this is done; a cutter for making leather washers to retain the oil in a wheel bearing. Maintenance tools for the heavier waggons and carts include the cart jack. A linch pin remover is necessary when a wheel is to be taken off for lubrication or

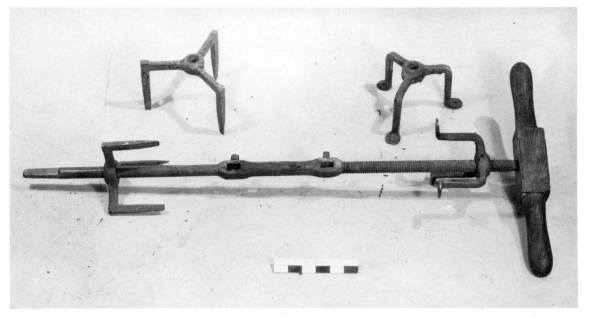

39 Boxing machine. Hand operated and adjustable; should also have a set of cutting blades. Used for boring out centre of nave to take iron boxes as used on older wooden axled vehicles

repair. The cart jack of the Kingsnorth shop has long ago been discarded, but the linch pin remover turned up – just where Dad had put it the last time it was needed. In his time the waggons coming up from the Romney Marsh to Ashford with their loads of wool bales or corn would often be halted at the shop to have all the wheels greased. The horses would remain in the shafts as the wheels were taken off and replaced; apparently they were too glad of a rest to want to move and upset the vehicle during maintenance, but it seems an unsafe sort of practice.

Woodland tools likely to be present in an old country shop include the barking irons, pit saws and the froe which is for light cleaving work. A timber jack is useful for moving large tree trunks, usually when stacking them. Ring dogs used with pole levers also help in moving large timber about in a yard or onto the sawpit. Timber dogs keep a trunk steady as it is sawn at the sawpit.

Most country wheelwrights also did general carpentry, and so the tools may include moulding planes. Perhaps the Victorian age accounts for there being such an extraordinary variety of moulding planes. These were used mostly in making window frames, also any fancy beading work. Hammers are inseparable from most ordinary carpentry. Handsaws, tenon saws, old frame saws, chisels and mallets also abound. Ladders were often made in old country shops, and needed special iron cramps to hold the work.

Morticing boxes help in gauging some pieces of work. Scribes, prickers and try-squares help to give accurate marking in woodwork. The awl starts a place for a drill hole. Rules are for ever in use, and are also a painful reminder of the present dilemma brought by the change to the metric system. This is especially apparent when repairing older houses; materials which are now standard are found to be too long or too short, too thick or too thin to match with the work.

Carpenters' trestles look so ordinary, but they are constantly in use for practically any woodwork job. The actual benches, too, are taken for granted, but they need to be solid and firm, and at the most suitable height for the worker.

A very large number of tools accumulate in any workshop, particularly when several generations have used the place, and it seems likely that some have been missed out in this account. There are also the many sundries such as nails, screws, bolts, staples, washers, each in a wide variety of sizes. The sundries, too, change with the times; old references mention 'clout nails', but these are no longer obtainable. There were once plenty of coffin nails in stock, and Bert remembers seeing an old tool box which had his great-grandfather's name made up of coffin nails on it – perhaps he had done it when still a boy.

Some other materials are reminders of old times: an iron pot containing pitch, which used to be heated up over a little fire, for pitching interiors of coffins and

40 Some tools for finishing and maintenance work. On left are the liner's palette, mahl stick and a paint knife. Centre is a bottle jack – so-called because of its shape. A leather washer cutter is next on right, and an adjustable coach spanner, two cap spanners and a linch pin remover

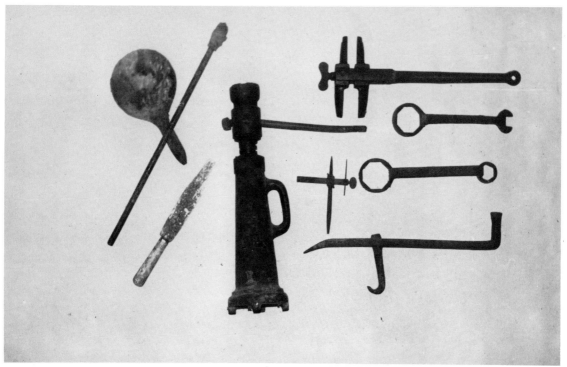

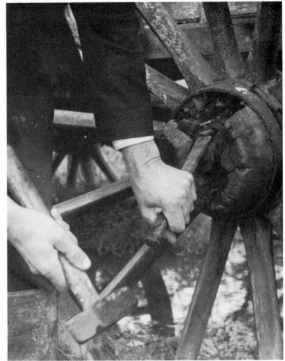

41   *Far left* Cap spanner in use. Many sizes, and the adjustable type also, were needed for maintenance work. The cap of a wheel was removed for oiling, or before the wheel was taken off

42   *Left* Loosening linch pin before using special tool to remove it. (*Courtesy of John Ferridge*)

43   *Left below* Lifting out the linch pin, using linch pin remover. The vehicle would need a cart jack placed under the axle whilst wheels were taken off for greasing or repair. (*Courtesy of John Ferridge*)

44   *Below* A group of woodland tools. (a) axe, (b) tree race or marker, (c) barking irons for flawing bark, (d) billhook, (e) froe, (f) iron wedges, (g) timber dogs, (h) ring dog, (i) cross-cut saw

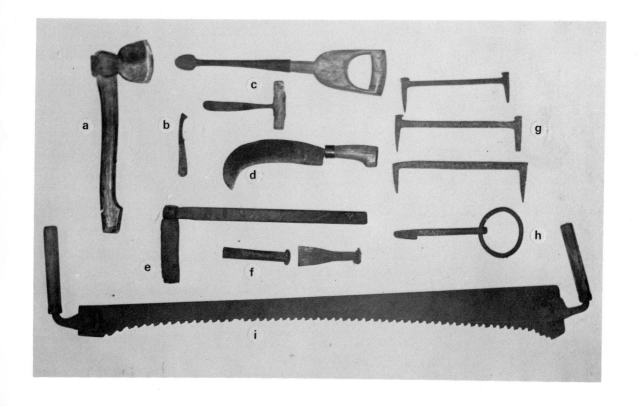

45   Beetle, a woodland tool, usually used for driving wedges when tree trunks are being split in the work of cleaving. (*In the museum collection of the Kingsnorth Trailer Company*)

46   Pitch pot (left) and glue pot hanging on overhead beam

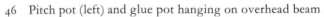

also sheep troughs; a piece of tallow which has crumbled away with age – and Bert cannot now remember its original purpose; a piece of Scotch glue. The tiny old glue pot has finally rusted away and fallen from its place on an overhead beam, but recently a good friend gave a replacement, so that this reminder can be preserved.

The painting of vehicles and other work is a matter of importance in a wheelwright's shop, and relics in the paint shop include the liner's palette and mahl stick still wedged behind a timber of the wall. The liner would visit the shop as required, probably walking out from Ashford. The story is that it was customary for someone to go down to the Queen's Head and buy a gallon of beer ready for the liner. When his hand was subsequently getting to the right degree of shakiness then he felt able to start, and the more shaky his hand the better the lines and other decorations would turn out. The brushes he used have disappeared, but it is said that they would just have a few straggly bristles or hairs. The art of lining was to get the paint at a suitable consistency so that it was good enough to get a strong impression, but liquid enough to draw the paint to a long line without lifting the brush away for replenishment. The whole scheme of lining was to obtain a good looking, but not showy, effect. Various colour combinations might be used when decorating a coachbuilt vehicle, but black lines were more likely on a cart or waggon.

47   Hop shim. An example of the implements once made in country shops.
(*Courtesy of John Gardner*)

CHAPTER 7

Carpentry and Other Work

THE COUNTRY wheelwright's shop was once the centre for just about anyone who needed something for the farm made of wood.

Farm Requirements

Strong barrows, York harrows and sheep feeding troughs have all been familiar things to Bert, though it becomes more difficult to contemplate making them these days, as any iron parts are usually made up by the blacksmith, if the product is to be in the traditional style.

In the farmyard itself the carpenter put up buildings – often using slabbing onto a wooden framework. Slabbing consists of the outside pieces sawn from a tree trunk, and is therefore flat on one side and elliptical on the other. Old sawpit and steam-sawing practice was to square up a trunk by sawing quite a thick piece of the outside away before carrying on with sawing the remainder into planks. These outside pieces were useful for cladding outbuildings, and a draught-proofed wall was achieved by applying another layer of slabs on the inside of a wall to cover the uneven joints left by the outside pieces. Modern sawmill practice is different in that the evenly spaced multiple saws go through the whole trunk rather like an egg slicer, and the outside pieces come away as waste.

The carpenter would have plenty of fittings to make for the interiors of farm buildings, e.g. mangers, feeding racks and partitions. Here the blacksmith also played a vital part by supplying large nails, bolts, brackets, hooks, chains, and even iron feeding racks.

The village craftsman made the wheelbarrows for both farm and garden use, and the wooden hames for horses' harness. Hand tools often needed new wooden handles. In some districts the carpenter made wooden pumps to draw up water from wells, and the main part of such a pump was made from an unseasoned elm trunk which had to be laboriously bored out from end to end.

Out in the fields there was more evidence of the work of both the carpenter and the blacksmith. The old wooden ploughs had numerous iron parts made by the smith. The Kent plough was a large, heavy tool, and certainly needed large, heavy horses to draw it. The clay soil of Kent and Sussex accounted for this design of

48   Horse and oxen ploughing. The wooden plough would have been made by the local carpenter or wheelwright. Aquatint by W.H. Pyne

49   'Model of the type of plough peculiar to Kent, built and widely used in this locality. Made in 1897 by Mr J.E. Eldridge, then aged 16 years, with some help from his father. At this time Mr Eldridge was working for Mr I. Tucker, carpenter and wheelwright of Hawkinge, who was a maker of these ploughs.' Exhibited at the Folkestone Museum. (*Courtesy of the Museum*)

plough. It must be many years since one of these was made in Bert's shop. He recently found a dust-covered piece of wood with pencilled marks to indicate the various measurement points along the main beam of a Kent plough. Also, he sometimes finds calves' teeth, or trent teeth, either in the shop or whilst digging the garden. These are oddly shaped nails, two of which are knocked into the end of a wooden spoke of a plough wheel to hold the trent in place. (A trent is the narrow-gauge iron tyre of an old plough or seed drill wheel.) Each spoke has an iron ferrule at the end, so preventing splitting of the wood.

Wooden harrows must have been made at some time or another in every country shop. In Bert's shop they have been made until fairly recent times, as the York and ordinary harrows remained useful even when drawn by tractors instead

50 One half of York harrow

of horses. (The York is a pair of harrows which are joined with iron fittings to make one.) On any wooden harrow there are plenty of iron fittings needed from the blacksmith – the tines, braces, and also the irons and chains to join up with the billets of the harnessing arrangement. The billet is one name for the wooden bar to which the horse's traces are attached and keeps the traces spaced away from the horse's body.

Early seed and fertilizer drills were made by the village carpenter in conjunction with the blacksmith, and were designed individually. The later patented drills often needed repair in the village shops. Some farm mowing machines can still require repairs which can be done in the village shop, as the connecting rod for the knife is made of wood for safety reasons, and it is a good thing to make a number of spares, together with the swathe boards which can also need renewing quite often.

Harvesting brought the waggons into full use as the loads of hay and corn were carried home. The root crops followed, and were loaded into the carts for transport to the storage places.

Ladders to enable the fruit crop to be harvested often came from the village carpenter's shop, although there used to be specialist ladder makers in some districts.

Wooden field gates are practical, and somewhat plain, but country carpenters used to find a special interest and satisfaction in making them. Selected oak is best, and the main joints are drawpinned – just as in waggon making. The hanging of a gate is an important part, and involves some deep digging to take the butt of the hanging post, as a good amount of post below ground helps in the successful life of a gate. Kissing gates are attractive and useful, and new ones continue to be made. The renewed interest in keeping footpaths open creates some of the demand for them. Stiles are another part of the rural scene; some being quite ordinary, whilst others are novel.

The following list of jobs, taken at random from the old account book of the Kingsnorth shop, gives some idea of the variety of local farm jobs expected of the village wheelwright and carpenter:

May 19th 1865	New Reast	1s. 0d.
,,	New Yeaks in Waggon B Wheels	9s. 6d.
,, 20th	Ringing 6 Willers Light Wheels	9s. 0d.
June 10th	New Beam in Plough	£1. 0s. 0d.
,, 26th	6lb. of Red Paint for Marking Sheep	4s. 0d.
Aug 4th	Drawing up Wheel and Showing Strakes	3s. 6d.
,, 17th	New 22 Stale Ladder	12s. 0d.
	Painting do.	2s. 6d.
Sep 4th	New Stump and Handles to Plough and paint	13s. 6d.
Oct 27th	Ringing Cart Wheel 6 Willers	18s. 0d.

Mar 21st	New Bottom Peace to Tail Board	1s. 9d.
Apr 1st	New Barrow	18s. od.
,,	Putting in Matock Helve	6d.

These entries seem brief when the amount of work involved is considered; for example, to put a new wooden beam to a plough would mean dismantling it and taking off a lot of iron fittings, and then renewing bolts, etc. as necessary when the plough was put together again with its new beam.

Household and General Work

The great variety of jobs which, even nowadays, are offered to a village shop lend a lively interest to the day-to-day work, and monotony is unknown. (The one real enemy is a long period of inclement weather; things do tend to grind to a halt then.)

The name 'wheelwright's shop' gives the impression that the daily scene was once centred around producing a continual succession of carts and waggons. In the case of the village shop this could not be the way at all, as the days were often filled with countless small jobs of repair and carpentry work, and the waggon building was fitted in whenever there was a lull in the day-to-day demands for other jobs. It took a long time to make a waggon and it would hardly fit into the needs of village life to carry on and complete a waggon to the exclusion of all other commitments. Orders for new waggons never came in large numbers, partly because the waggons lasted for a long time, and partly because the farmers who lived through the bad times would not be able to afford to order a new vehicle until absolutely necessary. A farmer who owned more than one waggon was the exception rather than the rule. When a waggon was ordered, it was understood that it would be some months or even a year before it was ready.

There was one circumstance, though, which did put all other considerations out of the way. That was when there was a death in the village. The carpenter was almost always the undertaker, and everything else in his shop came to a standstill whilst the coffin was made to measure and the formalities of a funeral arranged.

Some further random entries from the old account book show a few likely household requirements, although many others were quite ordinary house and garden repair jobs:

May 20th 1865	New Flower Stand & Painting, Varnishing	12s. od.
July 29th	Altering Door to Conservatory. Paint & Putty	1s. 3d.
Aug 29th	New Skirt Board for Ironing Dress	3s. 6d.
Apr 10th 1866	Blind Roles	1s. 6d.
Nov 24th	Repairing Writing Desk New lock & Hinge	1s. 8d.
Sep 16th 1867	New Clothes Box	10s. od.
Jan 6th 1870	New Butter Stool	5s. od.
May 16th 1869	New Hoop to Brine Tub & Pitch	2s. 6d.

51   Record photograph of stairs made in the shop to fit in an old farmhouse for room to room access. Bert and daughter Pauline

During the course of the present century the work naturally moved away from horse-drawn vehicle making and repairs, and wheelwrights had to turn to general carpentry for households and farms. Some decided to concentrate on building work.

Exterior and interior decorating is another addition to the range of work taken on. Dad never used to feel very happy when doing indoor work as it was so different from his previous experience. Bert, however, finds it congenial. Over the years a pleasant relationship develops with customers who regularly have household decorating, carpentry and fitting work done, and many of Bert's happiest hours have been spent working at the homes of those customers.

Undertaking

To many people the consideration of the practical work involved in undertaking is creepy and worrying, but within the household of a village carpenter it would have to be faced up to in a sensible way by all members of the family. Thus, Bert remembers how Mum used to arrange the swansdown lining of a coffin and make the little pillow; she would also boil up kettles of water ready for the special work of bending the side panels of a coffin. This laminated effect was obtained by making a series of sawcuts across the grain of a plank at the shoulder position of the coffin panel. Boiling water is poured onto the wood there, and the foot end can then be gradually levered up and supported with wood blocks, the head end of the plank itself being firmly braced onto the work bench. An angle gauge gives a guide as to when the bending is sufficient.

In the days of the village carpenter, each coffin was made to measure. Dad would take a piece of tape to the house of the deceased. A knot was made for the width and another for the length needed. Once, when there had been more local deaths than Dad could cope with in the necessary time, he went to a town concern to purchase a coffin. The proprietor told Dad that tape for measuring was out of date, and a folding rod was the thing; only country people still used tape. Dad's typical reply was that if someone was using it, then it wasn't out of date. He also found that individual measurement had been dispensed with, and so he had to choose from small, medium or large, none of which was quite right as far as he was concerned.

One day some undertaking duties found Dad and Bert at the hospital mortuary, where two men from another undertaker's were also on a mission. The younger of these decided to have a peep at the various occupants of the mortuary, and reeled off comments as to how peaceful they looked, etc. This came to an end after a quick look under one of the drapes, and an ashen-faced, silent young man hurriedly finished his work and left the scene.

The wood for coffins was usually oak or elm, according to the relatives' choice. Oak was more expensive. Thickness was another choice, one inch being the average decision. Furnishings, such as the ornate handles and beading were also

52   Using a piece of waste glass as a scraper to produce a fine finish to wood, as described for coffin making. The wavy marks on this piece of oak are a sought-after characteristic often known as the 'flower'

a matter to be discussed. The carpenter always liked to choose from his stocks the planks which had the best grain markings, and worked hard in every way to make the coffin beautiful. An old-fashioned method to bring a fine finish to the natural wood was to carefully scrape over the entire surface with pieces of waste glass. A piece of about six inches square was snapped off, and a slightly bulging edge of it was used as a scraper and replaced with a fresh piece as necessary. When the coffin had been assembled it was treated with linseed oil which gave the wood a lovely sheen and emphasized the grain markings.

The horses and carriages were, more often than not, from the Saracen's Head livery stables in Ashford. There was close involvement for the village undertaker, as he would have almost certainly known the deceased person as a fellow villager.

Something like twelve funerals a year were the average, but February was usually the busiest month for this work. Bert's mother always said that a person had not managed to 'get up February hill' whenever a death occurred during that month.

The old account book tells a little of these sad happenings, and the following are interspersed amongst the more everyday matters:

Dec 5th 1865	Small Coffin Best Furniture	£1. 5s. od.
,, 26th	Full Size Coffin	£2. 2s. 6d.
Jun 7th 1866	Fully Furnished Coffin	£3. os. od.
Feb 22nd 1868	Child Coffin	13s. od.

Some of the coffin prices have been altered to a lower figure; the carpenter often encountered extreme poverty and a family quite unable to meet the normal charges.

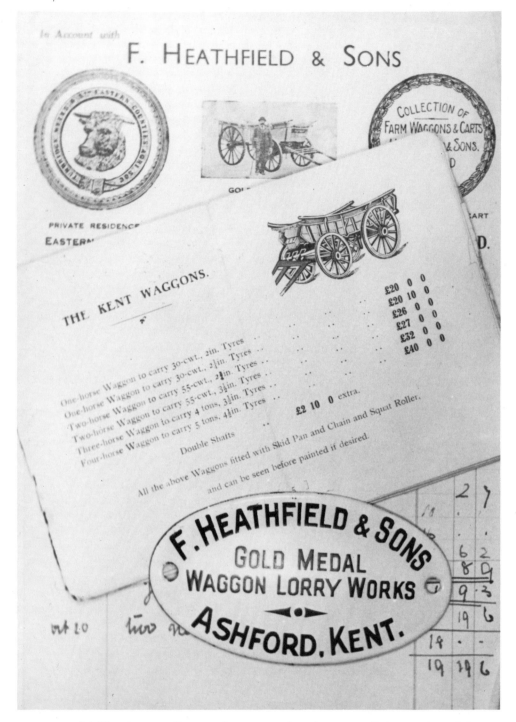

53   A billhead, a page from catalogue *c.* 1916, and an enamelled nameplate of the Heathfield concern. (*Courtesy of the Heathfield family*)

CHAPTER 8

Some Local
Wheelwrighting History

APART FROM being amongst the few village shops to have survived to the present time, the Kingsnorth shop has no particular claim to be the subject of a book such as this. Bert can remember some of the names of the wheelwrights in and around Ashford: Mr Sands, Willesborough; Mr Marshall, Smeeth; Mr Bingham, Shadoxhurst; Mr Link, Newchurch; Mr Crust, Bilsington (a stepson of Bert's grandfather) and Mr Heathfield, Ashford. In the main, the small village shops were similar in many ways to the Kingsnorth shop in so far as the type and output of work was concerned, with each craftsman jealously guarding his reputation for high standards of workmanship, and the experiences of each would have made a book of wide scope.

An example of the carpentry work of the late Mr Link, wheelwright, of New-church is to be seen in the little parish church of St Mary's-in-the-Marsh; the altar and the four riddell posts were made by him in 1947 from oak which he himself had felled and then seasoned in his yard for some fifteen years.

The elm chopping block in Bert's shop, which came from Mr Heathfield's Godinton Road Works, suggests the idea that a closer study of the Heathfield family's involvement in country wheelwrighting would give a view of a larger shop geared more exclusively to vehicle building than to all the general work expected of a small village shop.

Mrs Bertha Heathfield, the widow of Norman (known as 'Bernard') Heathfield, and Eric, their son, have kindly assisted by lending material and thus it is possible to record here some notes on this busy family concern. Bert remembers Bernard very well, as also would many farming families, in addition to the many new friends he made when he gave up the wheelwrighting and worked in an Army Ordnance Department. He died on 9 April 1975.

The outstanding thing about the two wheelwrighting generations of this family was that they loved the vehicle-building work to the extent that they expanded it and specialized in it. Francis Heathfield, Bernard's father, originally ran a concern known as the Weald of Kent Waggon Works at Headcorn, and gained a Gold Medal for waggon building at the Tunbridge Wells Show, c.1896, and later at the Bath and West Agricultural Show. He moved to Ashford at around the turn of the century to Godinton Road, where the works became extensive and always busy. Although some machinery for the basic woodworking processes like sawing and planing was installed, the actual building of each vehicle was all hand-done despite the large number of orders executed. The smithing was also done by traditional methods on the premises.

In a magazine article written in 1948 it was recorded that the Heathfields had, by then, built very many waggons and carts as well as vans, fruit and other carts. It was also stated that King George V liked the 'southern' type of waggon and several of the Heathfield models were bought for use on the Royal farms at Sandringham.

The love of good timber seems inherent in a wheelwright's make-up. Eric remembers that, when he was a youngster, he used to wonder why some special planks had been put aside in the timber stocks. Curiosity got the better of him and so he enquired, and was informed that his grandfather had selected them to be used for his own coffin when that was required. Strangely enough, his grandfather was actually at his wheelwrighting work when he died, suddenly and peacefully, whilst painting a wheel.

The list of customers who had waggons or carts made or other work done at the Heathfield works is extensive and covers a wide area, but always the family preserved the methods of practically everything being done by hand on traditional

54   An illustration from the catalogue *c*.1916 of F. Heathfield and Sons. (*Courtesy of the Heathfield family*)

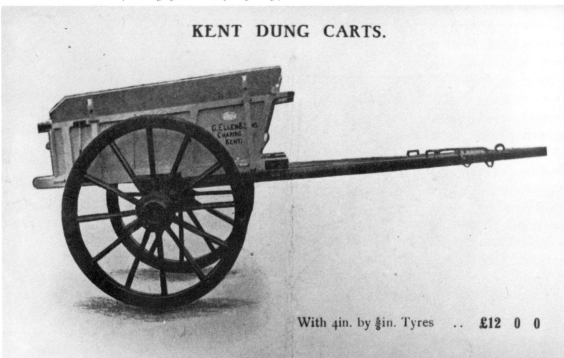

KENT DUNG CARTS.

With 4in. by ⅝in. Tyres   ..   £12 0 0

lines, and so they remained country wheelwrights in every sense. It is an interesting point that a neat little enamelled nameplate was usually affixed to the Heathfield vehicles, and this now makes identification much easier for anyone coming across a specimen. It is often a matter of difficulty to decide upon the maker of a vehicle, as so few ever had the builder's name in a permanent form, for, even if the name was painted on, it tended to fade with time.

Today, Eric runs a joinery concern, but amidst the up-to-date woodworking plant installed in his shop, he still hangs his father's drawknife over his bench as a reminder of the old family skills in wheelwrighting.

Ashford itself continues to hold a very strong position in the world of wheelwrighting, as the firm of Croford, Coachbuilders, Ltd. in Dover Place is one of the few remaining places qualified to meet almost any demands in the repair and restoration of all types of horse-drawn vehicles, as well as making various new products. Work on old vehicles comes to them from many parts of the world, as well as the UK, and includes the repair of wooden wheels used on early motor cars.

Croford's also hold a part of wheelwrighting history in some examples of wheelmaking machinery obtained when Headley's (Ashford) Wheel Works closed in the 1960's. Some of these machines date from the turn of the century, and were designed with great ingenuity.

Enthusiasm is something which is very apparent at Croford's, and the younger workers too are proud of the fact that the work they do is a part of history.

55   Jim Rootes

CHAPTER 9

Meet the Blacksmiths

T HE SKILL of the blacksmith was essential to the wheelwright. 'Like brothers,' one elderly countryman described the relationship. Therefore, this chapter pays tribute to the blacksmiths.

The forge of Kingsnorth has given way to garage premises, now run by the son of the former blacksmith and a partner, so it is good to have such close links with past times.

Nowadays, anyone who requires blacksmithing services must usually look outside his own village. For wheel work from the Kingsnorth shop, Jim Rootes comes to the rescue. His forge is several villages away, but he has helped Bert with wheel jobs in recent years. Jim has taught a number of apprentices over the years. Like Bert, he is probably the last of his family to practise the old family craft.

The following extracts from *The Rider* of 31 May 1974, quoted by kind permission, are from the series 'In the Country with Ivor Warne', which now appears in *The Kentish Express*.

BLACKSMITH'S TRADITIONS GO BACK 485 YEARS

Ask many older country lovers what they miss most and back will come the reply 'The village smithy'. However, there are still a few about.

I went in search of one the other day and found it not far from Ashford, in fact in the heart of Romney Marsh. Mind you it is not often the blacksmith is there for he is really what you might call a travelling smith.

But what a character when you meet him and can persuade him as I did to leave the forge where he was making sets of shoes to take to his customers over the next few days, and talk to me.

Jim Rootes comes from a family which have been blacksmiths for 485 years in the Biddenden, Frittenden, Pluckley areas and in the past century on Romney Marsh.

He told me: 'My father Arthur, he is now buried up the road in Newchurch Parish Church yard, worked on Romney Marsh for 68 years. He first worked for a smithy at New Romney then he came here where he was for 50 years. I was 12 when we came here. I went to the village school and when I got home used to help father "lump up" the shoes with a sledge hammer for the big cart horses.

'When I started we used to reckon on doing 180 cart horses for regular customers; some of them needed a new set of shoes two or three times a year.

'Now I am down to only two. One pulls a gypsy caravan as a novelty for a Marsh family and the other is at Hythe which works on a nursery. All my work today is with hunters and ponies within a radius of about 15 miles. I have about 245 regular customers, besides being official farrier to various groups.

'I do about 40 horses a week, averaging a 12- to 14-hour day. I often make the shoes up I shall require the next day when I get home at night. You are lucky to catch me in. This is the first time I have been at the smithy in the morning for about seven or eight months. It takes me on average three quarters of an hour to make a set of shoes and another three quarters of an hour to put the set on the horse.

'I do a bit of work on a Saturday. There is always someone who has got a pony wants seeing to and Sunday mornings I also do a bit. My wife, Winifred, we have been married for 24 years, will help me drill and tap the shoes.

'I have only had four holidays in my lifetime. Up to seven years ago we had not had a holiday. There was never time. We had a holiday last year.' If you can get Jim to talk about his earlier days, when instead of the present electrically-heated forge there was the Christmas card image of the bellows-driven glowing embers and the great lumbering cart horses waiting in a queue outside to come in for new shoes, he has some fascinating stories to tell.

Here is one. 'When it was a wet day at harvest time you knew you would have a busy day. You could look out of the window at 6.30 a.m. and see four or five cart horses waiting to come in the forge to be shod. Then you said: "I'll have a good breakfast first" because you knew it would be eight or nine o'clock at night before you would be able to stop for a meal.'

After an accident, Jim's father lost his nerve, so Jim had to learn early. Shoeing present-day hunters he describes as 'a bit of cake'. He remembers when cart horses were not broken until they were five years old and were almost wild.

He says horses are broken in much earlier today and are quieter than the days of the heavy horse.

Looking through old accounts Jim says he found his grandfather, Tom, used to charge 2s. 8d. a set for cart horse shoes. Today a set of shoes for a hunter comes to about £4 a set plus VAT which shows that even blacksmiths have got caught up with rising prices. Jim used to make a set of hunter's shoes for 6s. he says.

Jim first started being a mobile blacksmith by taking himself and his gear round with him in a motorbike and box sidecar. He now does it more in style in a motorvan.

George Stagg is a retired blacksmith who lives in a neighbouring village to Kingsnorth, and through him it is possible to learn some more of the blacksmithing experiences of former days. He was apprenticed to the craft at Saltwood, near Hythe in Kent, where he now finds that there is a garage on the site of the old forge, and the village pond where he remembers cooling the newly tyred wooden wheels has since been made into a car parking area. After apprenticeship he came to Ashford and worked for Mr Lawrence, who had a forge in Wellesley Road. George had lodgings near there at first, but later lived in a village about seven miles from Ashford and cycled to and fro.

Many memories of his blacksmithing days come to light as he talks of those busy times. He can remember using wrought iron before mild steel became generally used. The wrought iron worked so easily – 'like butter,' he says.

He always liked to make up sets of horseshoes and keep well stocked up in readiness for the arrival of the horses, but sometimes after a busy day there might not be time. Therefore, in the morning there could be several waiting whilst he toiled at the work of making up each set of shoes. 'Come on George, we want to get off,' grumbled the drivers with impatience.

The work of the larger concerns in the town seems to have been shared amongst the forges. The council had the largest horses, and the smiths nicknamed them 'the elephants', then there was quite a number of horses from the Saracen's Head livery stables. The breweries, Davis Timber Merchants, Pledges Flour Mills, Joint Stock Bakeries and many others all had horses, of course. On the Tuesday market days the farmers who came into the town often left their horses at the various livery stables, and sometimes they left a horse at the forge for shoeing attention and asked if it could be led back to one of these stables. One day George was taking one such horse back after shoeing, and it smartly kicked and smashed the window of Knott's shoe shop, then in Station Road. Everyone was chaffing, saying he would not get any wages that week with a window to pay for. However, it turned out that his employer had insurance against happenings like that.

Around 1910 the prices for entire shoeing were four shillings and sixpence for carriage horses, three shillings and sixpence for ordinary horses and ponies and five shillings and sixpence for farm and draught horses.

A little while before the Second World War George collected some tiny Shetland ponies from a stable in Dover Place. They belonged to the advance publicity section of Bertram Mills circus, and pulled a little stagecoach around a town as an advertisement. The man in charge said they would behave like lambs, and if they did not, to just tell them to stop it. The ponies were so small that it was necessary to kneel down to be able to shoe them, and George said he had never ached so much in his life as on this occasion. However, there were some complimentary tickets for the show, and he cycled home, had a quick cup of tea, put his little son on a cushion tied to the crossbar of his cycle and returned to Ashford to see the circus. Although his son has since travelled across the world several times, George says he still remembers the wonderful thrill of that circus visit.

George remembers so many of the old blacksmithing jobs. Setting a scythe and fixing a handle and doles is an example. The top dole was fixed at a height measured from the underarm to the fingers, and the lower dole at a further measurement from the elbow to the knuckles. The charge for a new, fully prepared scythe was seven shillings and sixpence. Gooseneck hoes, thistle packers, two-pronged Canterbury hoes, three-pronged hop garden spuds are all things he remembers making.

He is in his eighties now, and leads a very busy life, and particularly likes gardening. He is a keen member of the Ex-Servicemens' organizations. He was a Sergeant Farrier in the First World War, and remembers that was the only time a horse really hurt him; he bore no ill feeling towards the horse which had sent him flying for several yards where he lay unconscious. 'It was my own fault, I forgot to tell him I was there,' he said, with the quiet acceptance of one who understands the horse's own instinctive fears, which were, in this case, already aggravated by conditions of war.

Today motorized transport has imposed itself so completely on our lives that the horse-drawn era of not so very long ago is increasingly difficult to imagine. Older country people can remember the big horses at every farm who would lean their heads over a field gate, hopefully waiting for a friendly word from passers-by.

The farm workers who cared for those horses were often legends in their own villages; they would invariably remain at the farm long after a hard day's work was finished to see that their charges were properly cared for in the way of food and general comfort. (Overtime had a different meaning in those days, in that it was usually unpaid.) The good waggoner or ploughman was a trusted companion of his horses and assured of team spirit from them.

The same understanding was also a vital quality in the blacksmiths who shod the horses. The horses would be very decided in their trust or distrust of individuals, and this would be even more marked in farriery; the blacksmith who strove to win the confidence of every horse in his locality would have an easier job in the long run. Today's farrier has just as much need to find the best way of reassuring his four-legged customers, and the steady flow of quietly spoken phrases from him is as much an art of farriery as the detailed knowledge of the anatomy of the horse's foot.

CHAPTER 10

George Sturt Country

$\mathbf{A}$NYONE who becomes interested in wheelwrighting history will, sooner or later, find that his thoughts often turn to that area of Surrey connected with George Sturt's life and writings. They will delight in visualizing those days of the horse-drawn vehicles, and think of the old road waggons making their way over the Hog's Back, with the inevitable halt at the Farnham shop when George Sturt's grandfather had a contract for their maintenance.

George Sturt was born in 1863 – the centenary of his birth was celebrated by

56   Another Surrey workshop not far from the Hog's Back, the old Wheelwrighting and Blacksmithing shop at Worplesdon. Len Primmer, the retired blacksmith partner, remembers the adjoining green being covered with horse-drawn vehicles awaiting repair and collection

Telephone No. 86 Farnham.

FIRE.— We do not accept liability for any injury which may be caused by Fire to any property entrusted to us for any purpose.

STURT & GOATCHER

MOTOR & COACH BUILDERS,

Farnham, Surrey

25th October, 1916,

Sidney Wheeler served his apprenticeship in our shops, and was giving every satisfaction as an improver when he left to extend his experience. He was already a fair all-round wheelwright at that time. He has since specialised in the building of commercial motor bodies, acting as foreman in that department in a flourishing shop; and from my knowledge of his intelligence and good sense I shold think him excellently qualified for such a position. Were I in want of a leading hand, I should think myself fortunate if I could secure the services of Sidney Wheeler.

George Sturt

proprietor of "Sturt & Goatcher."

57   Testimonial from George Sturt for Sydney Wheeler. (*Courtesy of Bob and Betty Wheeler*)

the issuing of a paperback edition of his book *The Wheelwright's Shop* by the Cambridge University Press.

He went to Farnham Grammar School, and then became a teacher there. The failing health of his father meant that he had to leave this post when he was 21 and take over the family wheelwrighting business in East Street, Farnham. He was later joined by a partner, William Goatcher. He remained a bachelor. In 1916 he suffered a paralytic seizure which disabled him physically, but his interests remained unimpaired. He died in 1927.

Authorship was a passion with him, and he wrote books describing life in and around his locality at the turn of the century, using the name of George Bourne – derived from the area called The Bourne where he lived. There were other books too, but *The Wheelwright's Shop* under his own name became the best known. He made no pretensions to being a practical craftsman himself, but in his capacity of being a family member and also the 'Guv'nor' he transferred all that he knew and saw and heard in that provincial workshop into a first-hand account of craft

58 Bob and Betty Wheeler of Guildford, whose father, Sydney, was one of the last of the wheelwrighting apprentices at George Sturt's Farnham shop

folklore which has proved to be a classic in its field – just as predicted by *The New Statesman* when it was first published in 1923.

His book, being so packed with minute and varied detail, could be described as a bible of old country life; small portions of the text are often enough to bring whole scenes of those times to life. A point to mention here is that the names relating to craft practice vary in different parts of the country; it will be noted, for example, that naves are called stocks in Sturt's book. But there need never be much confusion about old references, as they were sensible and usually self-explanatory. Typically, George Sturt's book includes a glossary; it even includes the term 'woodlouse', referring to a small blood blister on the hand, so often suffered when using hand tools.

Today many links with that former wheelwrighting concern at Farnham can be traced. Descendants of those who worked there are proud of these associations, as are the descendants of Freddy Grover, who was the gardener at George Sturt's Vine Cottage home. Sydney Wheeler, for example, was one of the last of the coachbuilding and wheelwrighting apprentices at the Farnham shop. His son, Bob, of Guildford, remembers being taken, as a child, to the Sturt home by his grandmother; and his daughter, Betty, still treasures some of his tools dating from those early apprenticeship days. Many of his tools were destroyed in a fire at one of his places of work, and a new set was obtained through insurance, but these were never quite the same to him as the older ones had been. The wheelwright's side axe is one of the treasured original tools. Sydney bought this by hard saving when still a boy, and it is ground to suit the fact that he was left-handed. It is in remarkably good condition and demonstrates the care he bestowed on his tools.

As with the master wheelwrights, the changes of this century brought equal difficulties and adjustments to journeymen in the craft, although their basic skills could often be well adapted to many kinds of work. In Sydney's case he had a long spell in the building of bodywork for commercial motor vehicles. After over 25 years he moved and became happily involved in the job of building bodywork for electrically-driven invalid chairs to individual requirements. This was satisfying to him, suited his perfectionist type of temperament, and was entirely in keeping with his coachbuilding skills. Alas, the 1939–45 War meant that work at this place had to be switched to the war effort, but he remained there until his retirement in 1957. He died on 6 January 1967 at the age of 82. His lifelong enthusiasm for his craft has left his family with a deep interest in matters relating to wheelwrighting, and also, of course, to all associations with George Sturt.

A waggon attributed to the Sturt and Goatcher shop was presented to Farnham Museum by the late Alan Tice, and is now on permanent loan at the Old Kiln Agricultural Museum, The Reeds, Tilford, near Farnham.

CHAPTER 11

Today

IN 1975 THE Worshipful Company of Wheelwrights made a list of the active wheelwrights' shops they had been able to locate in England and Wales. Just over fifty shops were found, and the distribution of these is shown in Fig. 60. Some are town coachbuilding concerns, whilst some are country workshops.

Although this network of wheelwrighting tradition continues to exist, the work programme of each shop must be far removed from that of the old days. The main need today is for renovations to old vehicles for collections, museums and private enthusiasts.

Apprenticeship into the craft is very sparse, and as the master wheelwrights retire it seems that the future practitioners may often have to be those who adapt a natural flair in craftwork to the problems peculiar to wheelwrighting. This idea would not suit the old school of thought, but in the modern world much respect is due to those who wish to use their handicraft skills in preserving the beauty and function of vehicles of the horse-drawn era. Such skills are, of necessity, now quite expensive to the customer, partly because of the time factor involved, and also because of the difficulties in obtaining materials, parts, etc., but the enthusiastic owner's subsequent pride in a well turned out vehicle has its own compensations.

The museum vehicle collections are a source of delight; some consist of farm vehicles, and some specialize in the coachbuilt class of vehicle. Horse and agricultural shows and similar events often give the chance of seeing horses and vehicles.

Model-making gives the hobbyist a means of producing scale models of all kinds of horse-drawn vehicles, either from individual working plans made up by measuring a full-size specimen, or from sets of plans bought from the specialists who form collections of plans to offer fellow enthusiasts. The keyword to these specialists is authenticity, as it is this which makes the subsequent model into a collectors' piece rather than a mere ornament of doubtful proportions. Many beautiful models of horse-drawn vehicles have found their way into museums.

It is always a delight to meet retired wheelwrights, although one can sense a note of sadness for them to have seen the changes which took away the need for their skills. But they are hardy souls, often with a philosophy of life which eludes those enduring the pressures of the rat-race age. They secretly know that a full

59   The heraldic arms of the Worshipful Company of Wheelwrights

idea of the hard work of the old days cannot really be imparted, just as the great sense of satisfaction in making useful things, working from the rough tree trunk to finely finished articles remains a secret belonging to a past age.

In 1975 the Worshipful Company of Wheelwrights brought the models of a retired village wheelwright, George Dutton of Bury, Lancashire, to London and exhibited them in St Andrew's Church, Holborn for a month. This collection consists of waggons and carts and also the tools and equipment of a village wheelwright's shop together with the other carpentry things often made by the country wheelwright, such as ladders and wheelbarrows. They are made of the same species of wood as is used in full-size work. The setting of this very beautiful restored Wren church lent a special atmosphere of peace and timelessness to this display of the country wheelwright's art.

George Dutton, a third generation wheelwright, formerly of Cuddington, Cheshire, recalls that the Great War conditions allowed children in some schools who had reached Standard VII to leave at age thirteen if they had jobs to go to, and so his first job was in the offices of a local creamery – his family having felt that it would be an advantage for him to gain experience in clerical work. However, he had always loved the tools and atmosphere of his family's wheelwright-

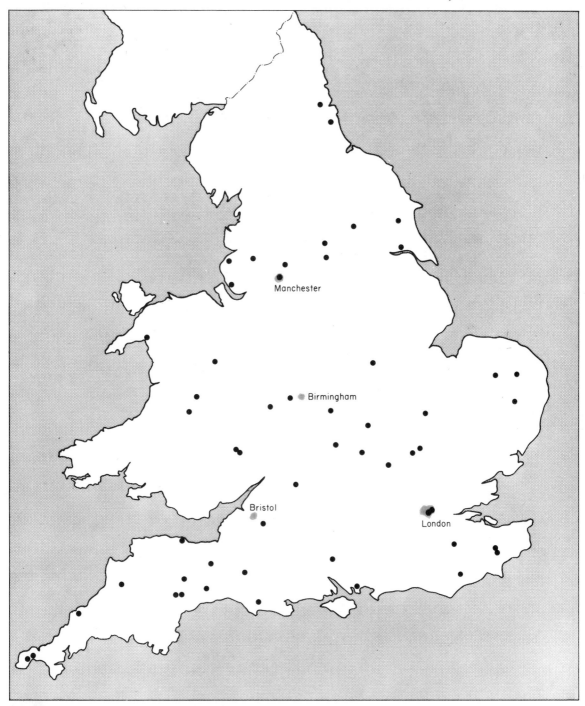

60   Map showing over fifty active wheelwrights' shops located in England and
Wales by the Worshipful Company of Wheelwrights in 1975. Quite a number are
country shops, still run by traditional wheelwrighting families

61   *Previous page* 1977, the Silver Jubilee Year of
H.M. Queen Elizabeth II. Servicing of the
vehicles taking part in the thanksgiving
procession was just one of the many preparations
involved, and this photograph shows the
re-tyring of a wheel from the Speaker's Coach
being done at Croford, Coachbuilders, Ashford.
Left to right Clive Bampton, Nicholas Gill and
Bob Bingham

62   Nicholas Gill cooling the fitted tyre

63   Don Wynder, signwriter, of Ashford, Kent, lining out a wheel as part of the restoration work of a museum piece

ing shop, and circumstances later enabled him to return and learn the craft. That same creamery provided a large part of the wheelwrighting work, with their milk floats and other horse-drawn vehicles, but eventually they became motorized, and George later decided to turn to the railway workshops where he worked on the repair of wagons, coaches, trailers and vans. Since his retirement, however, those old wheelwrighting memories have meant a great deal to him, and he has found much satisfaction in making the models which are destined for posterity.

The Story behind a Museum Exhibit

Quite a number of museums have exhibits of wheelwright's shops, complete with tools and equipment, whilst some have stored material of the craft. It is proposed here to look a little more closely at the story behind one such exhibit.

Walking around the grounds of the Weald and Downland Open Air Museum at Singleton, West Sussex, the visitor will come upon the wheelwright's shop set up near the Southwater forge. The great wheel and other typical equipment are reminders of the industry of the wheelwrights who formerly used them. However, when Arthur Plewis sees this particular exhibit his memory returns to the days when the 'Guv'nor' taught him the secrets of this woodland craft, and of the busy days at High Halstow, near Rochester in Kent, when these very tools were housed in the old church barn there. Fifty years of wheelwrighting memories come to his mind, but Arthur is a practical man, not given to useless sentimentality, and since his retirement in 1971, when he saw the several lorry loads of wheelwrighting equipment disappear down the road on their journey to Sussex after he had donated them to the museum, he has not wasted time on sadness. Instead, he has written a journal of his years in the craft, and made many drawings illustrating points of his craft, and the things made or repaired in that old barn workshop. He has also made models to show the design of carts, waggons and Kent ploughs once made in his village shop. It was an answer to his prayer that the arrangements for the tools and equipment to go to the museum arose following a televised news item about his retirement. The old barn workshop itself was demolished soon after, and homes for the elderly built on the site. He later gave assistance when it became possible for the wheelwright's shop exhibit to be set up in an old stable acquired by the museum.

His journals show that he was apprenticed at the age of fourteen to David Harryman ('the Guv'nor') in 1921 and settled well to the craft of village wheelwright and carpenter. After the concern had changed hands to a new 'Guv'nor', Arthur himself eventually took over, and he was always a busy craftsman. Neither did he escape the rigours of undertaking work. How well he remembers the dreadful weather which accompanied quite a few of the funerals; each detail is stamped upon his memory, because he often dug the grave as well as made the coffin, and saw to the formalities. He remembers, ruefully, how it was always an easy matter to get volunteers as bearers for a funeral, but there was never a rush

Wheelwrights

GOD GRANT UNITY

Although their trade had been established for many centuries it was not until 1630 that the wheelwrights of London first applied to the City authorities for incorporation. However they were only granted their charter in 1670 during the reign of Charles II and did not receive the right to bear a livery until 1773.

Originally the Company was vigilant in its control of the wheelwrights' trade and imposed heavy penalties on those guilty of shoddy workmanship or use of inferior materials. It also supported destitute company members and the widows and orphans of former brethren. However by the late eighteenth century the company ceased to exercise authority over the trade which was carried on nevertheless in villages and towns throughout Britain.

From 1882 onwards the Company has made generous use of its limited funds to further technical education and to keep alive the spirit of craftsmanship although the trade itself has almost vanished.

This exhibition celebrates the life work of one of the last village wheelwrights, George Dutton, who was made a Freeman of the Worshipful Company of Wheelwrights in 1975.

64   *Left* The introductory inscription for the 1975 exhibition in St Andrew's
Church, Holborn

65   *Above* Some of the equipment of a village wheelwright's shop in model form,
made by George Dutton, retired wheelwright, of Bury, Lancashire, and seen here
in St Andrew's Church, Holborn, at an exhibition, 'The Wheelwright's Art',
organised by the Worshipful Company of Wheelwrights in 1975

66   Model by George Dutton, at the 1975 exhibition

67 Arthur Plewis with cart and waggon models he has made in exact replica of
the full-sized vehicles once made in his North Kent workshop

of assistance at the actual 'coffining' of a body.

Arthur was happy when he, in turn, took on an apprentice. Always, a special
bond existed between a master and his apprentice, perhaps rather like that of a
father and son.

The drawings are detailed and technical, and done entirely from memory. A
few are reproduced in these pages, and they illustrate both the scene of the old
barn workshop and the detailed interest of various points of the craft. These
drawings and the journal form an unpublished collection and at present are
planned to be used as museum archival material.

The tool and equipment collection is of unusual completeness. Arthur never
threw anything away from the old barn workshop, and the history of that place
was already old-established when he first went there as an apprentice. Even the
old oil lamps were saved, as well as old tin containers, a paint mill and countless
other small items no longer likely to be seen. He was meticulous in the care of the
tools, even those which were already worn away with use. The old chopping

68   The scene of the village wheelwright's shop at High Halstow, 1921. Drawn from memory by Arthur Plewis

block was one particular item for special care, and if anyone should thoughtlessly rest a foot on it he could have cheerfully amputated the offending foot, for he did not want any grit and dirt transferred to the block to spoil the razor sharpness of the axes.

Discipline and hard work have been keynotes in his life. From earliest days he was taught to help at home, having to get up very early to see to several chores before he set off to walk to school. That walk to and from school was always a nature trail to him; no wild life or living plant escaped his eye. During leisure moments he liked to sit high up in a tree observing the wild life of the then lonely North Kent marshes. In later years the study of wild life has been just as absorbing to him, and whenever he saw various-sized lumps of wood shavings move across the floor of the barn workshop it indicated that all was well with the hedgehog family living there; they invariably got the shavings entwined on their prickly bodies and looked very comical as they journeyed across the shop.

THE WHEELWRIGHTS BENCH AND PAINT CORNER

TODAY

69   *Previous page* The wheelwright's bench and tools, and the paint corner at the barn workshop, High Halstow. A memory drawing by Arthur Plewis

70   *Below* Another view of the former workshop, as seen from the main doors. This area was where the waggons and largest implements were built. To the left, carts and vans. The bench to the right was the joiner's

71   *Right* North Kent waggon as made in the High Halstow shop.
72   *Right, below* North Kent farm cart, in the design of those made in the High Halstow shop

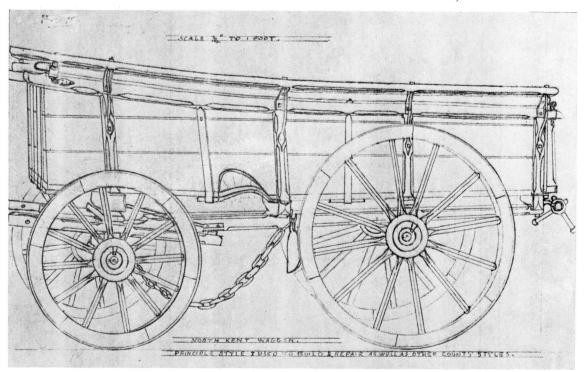

SCALE ¾" TO 1 FOOT.

NORTH KENT WAGGON.
PRINCIPLE STYLE & USED TO BUILD & REPAIR AS WELL AS OTHER COUNTY STYLES.

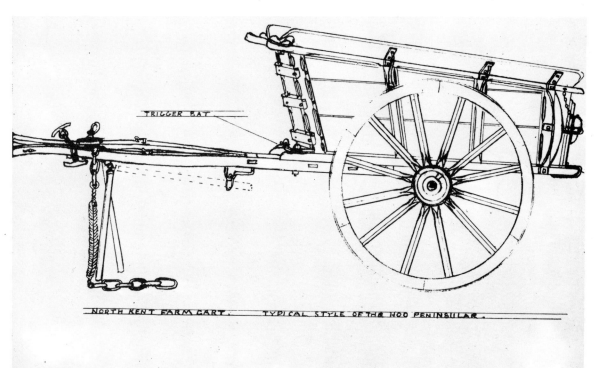

TRIGGER BAT

NORTH KENT FARM CART.   TYPICAL STYLE OF THE HOO PENINSULAR.

73   The samson and straking details drawn by Arthur Plewis

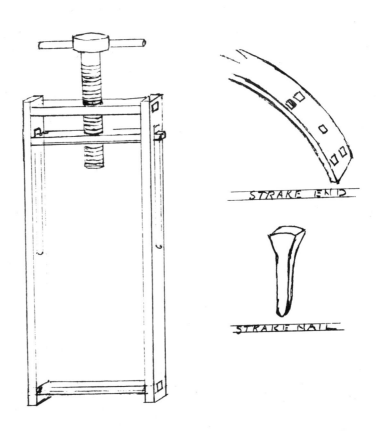

STRAKE END

STRAKE NAIL

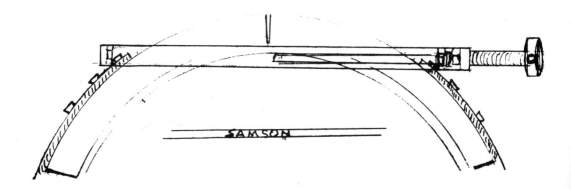

SAMSON

74 *Left* The 'great wheel' to drive the wheelwright's lathe, originally at the High Halstow shop. (Wheelwrighting collection, Weald and Downland Open Air Museum.) (*Courtesy of the Museum*)

75 Part of the paint corner in the wheelwright's shop exhibit, Singleton. This can easily be recognised in Arthur Plewis' drawing of his old barn workshop, Fig. 69. (*Courtesy of the Museum*)

76 *Left* Old paint mill seen in the wheelwright's shop exhibit; Arthur Plewis remembers grinding pigment and paint skins in this mill. The 'Guv'nor' would examine the result, and invariably the adjustments would have to be tightened down and the powder again put through. (*Courtesy of the Museum*)

77, 78, 79 *Below* Cart and waggon jacks. (Wheelwrighting collection, Weald and Downland Open Air Museum.) (*Courtesy of the Museum*)

80   Tyre bender. (Wheelwrighting collection, Weald and Downland Open Air Museum.) (*Courtesy of the Museum*)

CHAPTER 12

The Heavy Horse

O N REVIEWING the compilation of this book, it can truly be said that the cart has been put before the horse! No such thing is intended, of course, as the horse is the *sine qua non* of everything discussed in the preceding chapters.

The twentieth century has seen an extraordinary fluctuation in the horse population of our country. The heavy horse, in particular, almost disappeared at one time – for in the mid-1960's it was considered that there were only just over two thousand left, whereas in the 1920's there had been about two million horses at work on the farms, roads and canal banks. The tide has begun to turn now, as quite a few farmers have discovered that there is still a place of extreme usefulness for the heavy horse on the farm amidst all the mechanized methods of today. The brewers have always nurtured the horse as part of their trade, but now they also find that there is often every good reason for increasing their number of work horses. In addition there is a surge of general public interest, and the enthusiastic work of various societies and individual owners is helping to bring the heavy horse back into its proper position of affection and usefulness.

Today the four main breeds of the heavy horse found in Britain are the Shire, Clydesdale, Suffolk and Percheron. Each of these breeds has a fairly clearly defined history, and much interesting information is to be found elsewhere and in handbooks issued by the Societies concerned. Membership is open to anyone interested in the heavy horse, not just to owners and breeders. Family membership is often encouraged, and the exciting events, such as shows and ploughing matches must make ideal family outings for those who enjoy country activities.

A flashback to show something of the draught horse picture at the end of the nineteenth century is given here by quoting fully the relevant section from *Modern Practical Farriery* by W.J. Myles, M.R.C.V.S.L. (*c.*1890).

THE DRAUGHT HORSE

Up to within these few years our principal employers of draught horses in the metropolis aimed almost exclusively at the procuring of those grand, stately, and immense animals which judicious crossing with the Flemish and old Suffolk Punch so often produced. Of late, however, the immense demand for a horse of higher activity and handiness, for the service of the railway van, has

given the waggon horse a stamp more approaching to the Cleveland, or the
'machiner' – a smart trot, as well as a sheer-strength pull, being a desideratum.
When the old 'sumpter', or carrier's horse, was used in England, for the con-
veyance of loads in packs or panniers, some of the Yorkshire sumpter horses
have been known to carry 700lbs. weight sixty miles in the day, and to repeat
this journey four times a week, while mill horses have carried 910lbs. for
shorter distances. This is the stamp of animal required by the Baxendales,
Chaplins, and Pickfords; another sort is yet the pride of our great brewers,
distillers, and London waggon owners. The remarks of a gentleman 'frae north
o' Tweed' on these horses are so genuine and apposite that we transcribe them:
'A prevalent error of strangers is that these magnificent horses are merely
meant as an advertisement of the firm to which they belong. The large and
opulent brewer has less occasion for this kind of publicity than any other
trader. His customers are compelled to come to him: a chance sale is a *rara avis*.
He has these horses because extraordinary exertion is sometimes required, and
he can command it when necessary: at the same time they are too valuable to
be uselessly worn out, and pay better in the long run for the attention bestowed
upon them. This has led many into the error of supposing these splendid
animals cannot do the work of such as, from want of proper points to command
the higher prices, get into the more laborious employments; and you will hear
the owners of these inferior horses constantly remarking on one of these
beautiful teams, as not only the pride of the drayman, who beckons them to
him like old acquaintance, and which they answer with the sagacity of bipeds,
but they are also the pride and admiration of all Englishmen, and the astonishment of most foreigners. A Scotchman is certainly not a foreigner, being but
an Englishman of a distant portion of Great Britain; but I cannot help noticing
that, when visiting the Land of Cakes, I have always felt elated at the animated
description of their feelings at first beholding these noble creatures. They were
full of astonishment, and could not tell which made the greatest impression,
their extreme beauty, vast size, sagacity, or docility, amounting beyond
parallel. One gentleman remarked, "I have been over most of the globe; I have
seen many of its wonders; but the greatest I ever saw was in London. I saw a
brewer's team lowering some butts of beer. The horse that performed this
office, without any signal, raised the butts, and returned and lowered the rope;
not a word or sign escaped the man at the top of the hole, who only waited to
perform his part as methodically as his four-footed mate did his. Two others
were sometimes playing at intervals in apparent converse. The cellaring
finished, the horse took his place by the team: the other loose horse, that had
been going wherever he pleased, also came, and was hooked on. The man
adjusted his dress, then walked away; the team followed. Not one word has
passed, not even a motion of the whip, or any other intimation of what was
to be done next." He added, he had never seen the same number of men work
in such unison with the various changes: it was wonderful, and if it was not

81   Suffolk Punch, Beccles Domain. Champion mare, Royal Norfolk Show,
7.8.53

reason, he thought the greater portion of mankind had better give up some
part of their reason to learn sagacity from a dray-horse. He continued: "I
followed some distance to see how it was that a man, who seemed as if he could
be crushed at any moment by these monsters, had such control over them. I
observed he never touched them: between carriages where there hardly seemed
room enough to squeeze through, he went without touching, and this, too, by
merely waving a bit of whipcord on the end of a long black rod." He finished
with – "I was quite astounded; it was truly wonderful; and I always recollect
the sight with pleasure; and can hardly prevail upon myself that it was not some
necromancer waving an enchanted rod.""

   This digression dismissed, we will proceed to show that the observation
that brewers' horses cannot do the more laborious kinds of work, particularly
that of town carmen, is a mistake. There is not often an opportunity of proving
the fact, the greater part of the brewers being too liberal to their old servants

to part with them when worn out: most of them, therefore, have them destroyed when, from old age or accident, they are incapacitated from performing their work with moderate comfort. Some wealthy gentlemen, aye, and ladies too, may take a leaf in this respect, at least, out of the brewers' book, when many a favourite hunter, charger, ladies' pad, hack, and even racer, will be saved the torture of dragging street-cabs and costermongers' carts with aching limbs, crippled feet, galled shoulders and back, for the sake of putting into the pocket of the seller not perhaps one half what the old dray horse would fetch.

There are a few exceptions of brewers selling their horses, and we feel confident all those who have bought them have found them work better than the ordinary horses at the same age. One was sold out from being supposed to be lame: he turned out sound. Three tons and a half, including his cart, became his ordinary load, and with this he went all over London and the neighbourhood, and never had, or required, any assistance, not even over the bridges, or up hills. He certainly was a remarkably fine horse, and kept up his fat till he died, some years after leaving the brewhouse.

82   Harness. Drawing by W.G. Simmonds at Ashford Market, Kent, 17.8.26

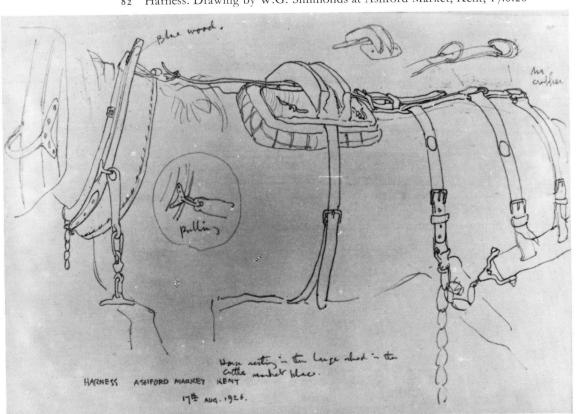

The heavy black horse, a favourite with the coal-merchants, is bred chiefly in the midland counties, from the fens of Lincolnshire to Staffordshire. Many are bought up by the Surrey and Berkshire farmers at two years old; and, being worked moderately until they are four, earning their keep all the while, they are then sent to the London market, and sold at a profit of ten or twelve per cent.

It would not answer the breeder's purpose to keep them until they are fit for town work. He has plenty of fillies and mares on his farm for every purpose that he can require; he, therefore, sells them to a person nearer to the metropolis, by whom they are gradually trained and prepared. The traveller has probably wondered to see four of these enormous animals in a line before a plough, on no very heavy soil, and where two lighter horses would have been quite sufficient. The farmer is training them for their future destiny; and he does right in not requiring the exertion of all their strength; for their bones are not yet perfectly formed, nor their joints knit, and were he to urge them too severely, he would probably injure and deform them. By the gentle and constant exercise of the plough, he is preparing them for that continued and equable pull at the collar which is afterwards so necessary.

The true Suffolk Punch, which did much for our best short-legged dray-horses, is not found now in its purity. It stood from fifteen to sixteen hands high, of a sorrel colour; was large-headed; low shouldered, and thick on the withers; deep and round chested; long backed; high in the croup; large and strong in the quarters; full in the flanks; round in the legs; and short in the pasterns. It was the very horse to throw his whole weight into the collar, with sufficient activity to do it effectually, and hardihood to stand a long day's work.

The present breed possesses many of the peculiarities and good qualities of its ancestors. It is more or less inclined to a sorrel colour; it is a taller horse; higher and finer in the shoulders; and is a cross with the Yorkshire half or three-fourths bred.

The excellence, and a rare one, of the old Suffolk – the new breed has not quite lost it – consisted in nimbleness of action, and the honesty and continuance with which he would exert himself at a dead pull. Many a good draught-horse knows well what he can effect; and, after he has attempted it and failed, no torture of the whip will induce him to strain his powers beyond their natural extent. The Suffolk, however, would tug at a dead pull until he dropped. It was beautiful to see a team of true Suffolks, at a signal from the driver, and without the whip, down on their knees in a moment, and drag everything before them. The immense power of the Suffolk is accounted for by the low position of the shoulder, which enables him to throw so much of his weight into the collar.

Although the Punch is not what he was, and the Suffolk and Norfolk farmer can no longer boast of ploughing more land in a day than any one else, this is undoubtedly a valuable breed.

The Duke of Richmond obtained many excellent carriage horses, with

strength, activity, and figure, by crossing the Suffolk with one of his best
hunters.

The Suffolk breed is in great request in the neighbouring counties of Norfolk
and Essex. Mr Wakefield, of Barnham, in Essex, had a stallion for which he
was offered four hundred guineas.

The Clydesdale is a good kind of draught-horse, and particularly for farming
business and in a hilly country. It derives its name from the district on the
Clyde, in Scotland, where it is principally bred. The Clydesdale horse owes its
origin to one of the Dukes of Hamilton, who crossed some of the best Lanark
mares with stallions that he had brought from Flanders. The Clydesdale is
larger than the Suffolk, and has a better head, a longer neck, a lighter carcase,
and deeper legs; he is strong, hardy, pulling true, and rarely restive. The
southern parts of Scotland are supplied from this district; and many Clydes-
dales, not only for agricultural purposes but for the coach and the saddle, find
their way to the central and even southern counties of England. Dealers from
almost every part of the United Kingdom attend the markets of Glasgow and
Rutherglen.

Professor Low (in his *Illustrations of British Quadrupeds*) says, that 'the
Clydesdale horse, as it is now bred, is usually sixteen hands high. The prevailing
colour is black, but the brown or bay is common, and is continually gaining
upon the other, and the grey is not unfrequently produced. They are longer in
the body than the English black horse, and less weighty, compact, and muscu-
lar; but they step out more freely, and have a more useful action for ordinary
labour. They draw steadily, and are usually free from vice. The long stride,
characteristic of the breed, is partly the result of conformation, and partly of
habit and training; but, however produced, it adds greatly to the usefulness of
the horse, both on the road and in the fields. No such loads are known to be
drawn, at the same pace, by any horses in the kingdom, as in the single-horse
carts of carriers and others in the west of Scotland.'

The important place of the horse in the everyday life of former years gave rise to
so many occupations, such as shoeing, harness making and saddlery and, of
course, the work of managing the horses by coachmen, carters, waggoners,
ploughmen and others. The town coachbuilders and the village wheelwrights
and carpenters have all played a vital part in that scheme of things, and no-one
with memories of being involved in those occupations harbours any regrets.

83   Plough teams. Hampnett, Gloucestershire, 1935

Bibliography

ARNOLD, J., *The Farm Waggons of England and Wales,* John Baker, 1969.

ARNOLD, J., *Farm Wagons and Carts*, David and Charles, 1977.

BAILEY, J., *The Village Wheelwright and Carpenter*, Shire Publications, 1975.

JENKINS, J.G., *The English Farm Wagon*, David and Charles, 1961.

ROSE, W., *The Village Carpenter*, EP Publishing, 1937.

STURT, G., *The Wheelwright's Shop*, Cambridge University Press, 1923.

THOMPSON, J., *Making Model Horse Drawn Vehicles*, 1976. (Available only from John Thompson, 1 Fieldway, Fleet, Hants.)

TOULSON, S., *Discovering Farm Museums and Farm Parks*, Shire Publications, 1977.

VINCE, J., *Discovering Carts and Wagons*, Shire Publications, 1970.

VINCE, J., *An Illustrated History of Carts and Wagons*, Spur, 1974.

Index

Numbers in **bold type** refer to the figure numbers of the illustrations.

119

Weathered veterans 5

Denis H. Somerfield

AT OLD KILN MUSEUM · TILFORD

Old Kiln Museum is an entirely private collection, assembled and run by Mr. and Mrs. Henry Jackson. It is pleasantly distributed over an area of ten acres of field, woodland and barns and comprises a large number of implements and devices marking over a hundred years of farming. The many aspects of the subject are here displayed with the obvious advantage of a rural setting. The wide variety ranges from carts, waggons and ploughs to yard machinery, including a hop press, to a complete wheelwrights shop, a working smithy, dairy equipment and even to tree culture and gardening exhibits.

A picnic area with rustic tables and benches is close by a shop where fresh, homegrown, fruit and vegetables are available in season. Souvenirs and books on country matters can be had here — and the car park is free.

OLD KILN AGRICULTURAL MUSEUM
REEDS ROAD · TILFORD
FARNHAM · SURREY
Frensham 2300

Tunwrest plough
Sussex 1870

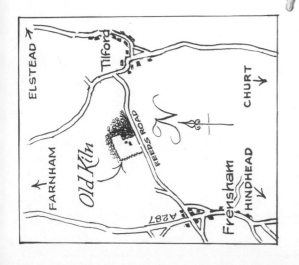

Old Kiln Museum is on Reeds Road half way between Frensham and Tilford. An official finger post at both ends of the road indicates "agricultural museum". Approximate distances between Old Kiln and three points of approach are Farnham 3 miles, Frensham Great Pond 2 miles, Elstead 3 miles.

Open Wednesday to Sunday (and Bank Holidays) from early April to late September — 11 o'clock until 6 p.m.

Schools and groups may make party bookings not less than one week in advance.

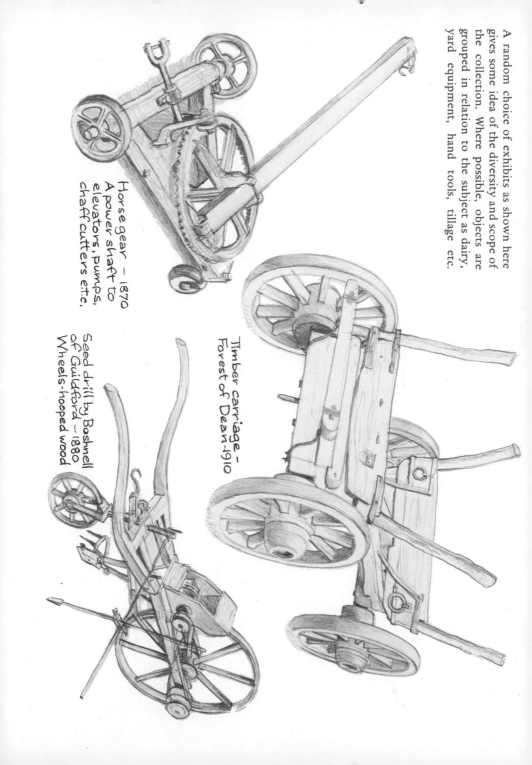

A random choice of exhibits as shown here gives some idea of the diversity and scope of the collection. Where possible, objects are grouped in relation to the subject as dairy, yard equipment, hand tools, tillage etc.

Horse gear – 1870
A power shaft to elevators, pumps, chaff cutters etc.

Timber carriage – Forest of Dean-1910

Seed drill by Bashnell of Guildford – 1880
Wheels-hooped wood

HAND TOOLS

This assembly of manual implements covers aspects of cultivation, sowing, reaping, hedging, ditching, tree felling, and allied trades as thatching and hurdle-making. Deceptively simple, requiring skill and stamina to wield, these are the tools that made the harvests possible, through many centuries of English farming.

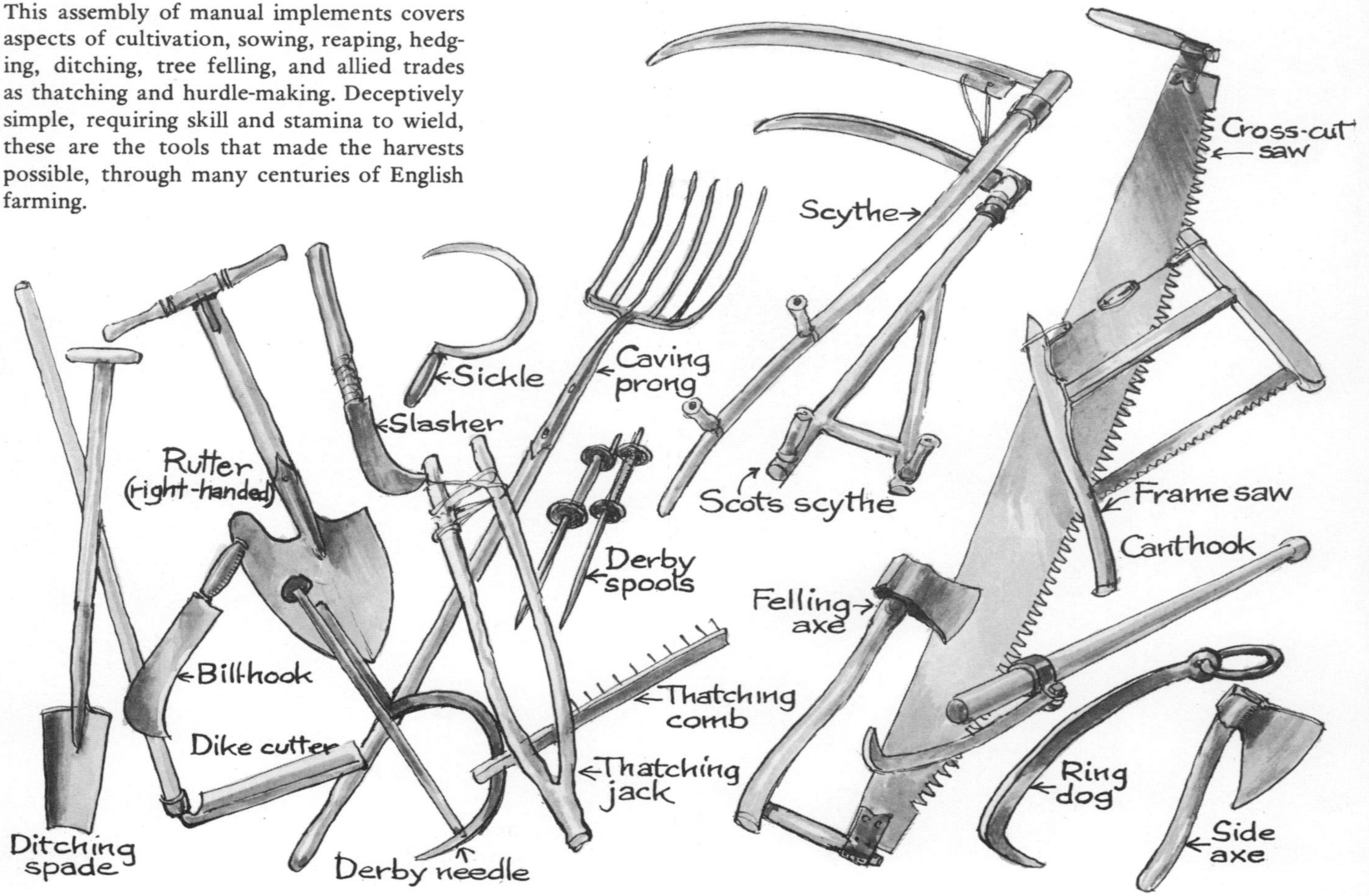

Cross-cut saw

Frame saw

Cart hook

Side axe

Ring dog

Scythe

Scots scythe

Felling axe

Thatching comb

Thatching jack

Caving prong

Derby spools

Sickle

Slasher

Derby needle

Rutter (right-handed)

Billhook

Dike cutter

Ditching spade

THE FORGE

Anvil, forge and bellows, with a formidable array of hammers and tongs for the smith to meet the many demands of the farm. His skill ranged from shoeing to the making of harness tugs, chains and rings to gate furniture and plough repairs.

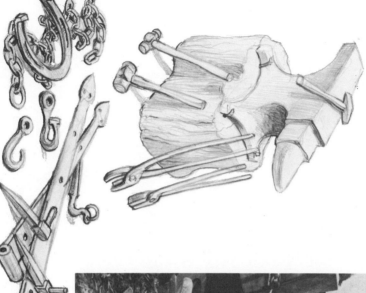

WHEELWRIGHTS SHOP

A live workshop in a state of pause. Wheels in the making, and benches astrew with tools, felloes and patterns. The mastery of wood is shown in the precision a true wheel exacts from the experienced craftsman.

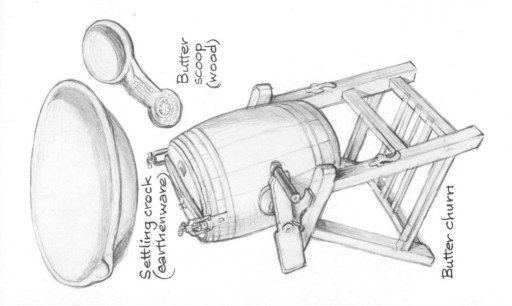

Butter scoop (wood)

Settling crock (earthenware)

Butter churn

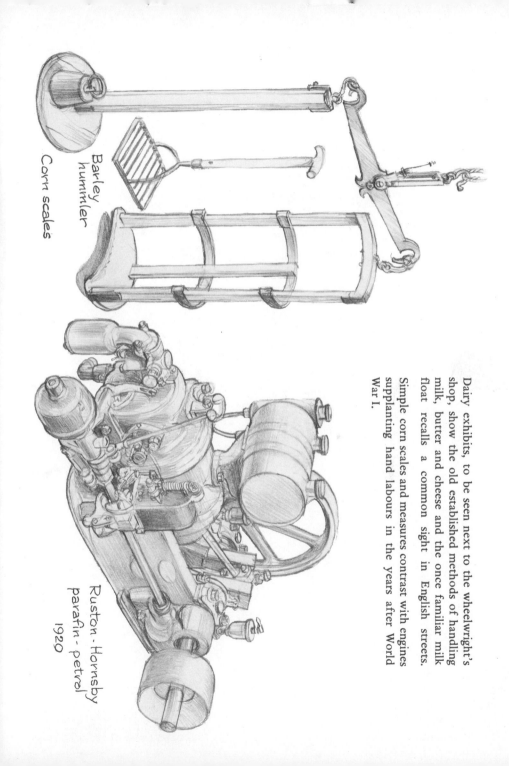

Corn scales

Barley
hummler

Ruston · Hornsby
parafin · petrol
1920

Dairy exhibits, to be seen next to the wheelwright's
shop, show the old established methods of handling
milk, butter and cheese and the once familiar milk
float recalls a common sight in English streets.

Simple corn scales and measures contrast with engines
supplanting hand labours in the years after World
War I.

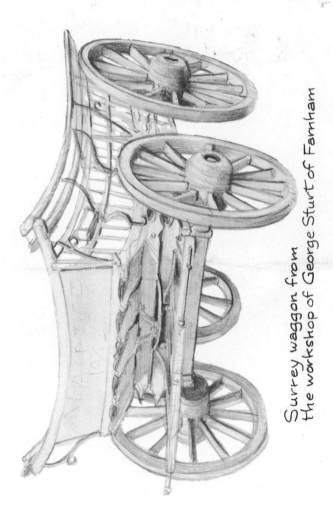

Surrey waggon from
the workshop of George Sturt of Farnham